'Claire Beeken's story is ██████████████████████████
repel you, but it's still on████████████████████████
ent – and every teenage█████████████████████████████
human spirit's ability to ████████████████████████████

'Once you begin reading ███ powerful and moving account
of Claire Beeken's struggle with anorexia, you can't stop ...
This frank and emotive story gives much-needed voice to
the ever-growing number of young people suffering from
eating disorders.'

Top Santé

'A challenging and insightful account...'

Publishing News

'Any eating disorder is a cry for help, and Claire Beeken
illustrates how she used food to try and regain the control
of her life that she was so clearly denied as a child. Having
survived near death, she tells her story with moving honesty
and insight and I read without stopping from start to finish.
I hope the account of her journey and determination to
understand this destructive compulsion will comfort and
help others'

Caryn Franklin, presenter of the BBC's *Clothes Show* and patron of
the Eating Disorders Association

'The world inside the head of an anorexic has never been
more honestly conveyed ... Claire's wit is her strength, and
this is a compelling, funny and insightful account of her
illness that has moved me beyond all belief.'

Diane Youdale, TV and radio presenter, and former Gladiator, 'Jet'

'Since your book, *My Body, My Enemy,* was published, we have placed it on our reading list, and it has been a great help to sufferers and a source of insight to those of us who are a long time in recovery.'

Letter from INEDA, the Irish Eating Disorders Association in Dublin, now known as *Bodywhys*

'One day I bought a book called *My Body, My Enemy,* it was the best book I ever read. After reading the book I realized just how much pain I was causing my body. Slowly but safely my weight has become more stable.'

Letter from a 15 year old sufferer in Denmark

I have just read your excellent book, *My Body, My Enemy,* which I found highly readable. It provided a fascinating (and sympathetic) insight into anorexia nervosa and how it affected you. I congratulate you on being able to overcome it and share your experiences with readers; and for your work in setting up the self-help group for other sufferers.'

Letter from a sufferer in Hertfordshire

'I have just finished your book *My Body, My Enemy.* I read it from beginning to end without it down. Unfortunately there is little help for me – being a male sufferer, and it's good to read of the services you provide for sufferers in your area.'

Letter from a male sufferer in Manchester

'Thank you so much for writing *My Body, My Enemy.* Reading your book has helped me have a better insight into my daugter's illness. We are now able to talk about her problems.'

Letter from a carer in London

My Body, My Enemy

My Body, My Enemy

My thirteen year battle with anorexia nervosa

Claire Beeken
with Rosanna Greenstreet

Thorsons

Thorsons
An Imprint of HarperCollins*Publishers*
77–85 Fulham Palace Road,
Hammersmith, London W6 8JB

The Thorsons website address is: www.thorsons.com

Published by Thorsons 1997
This updated edition 2000

3 5 7 9 10 8 6 4 2

© Claire Beeken and Rosanna Greenstreet 1997, 2000

Claire Beeken and Rosanna Greenstreet assert the moral right to be
identified as the authors of this work

A catalogue record for this book
is available from the British Library

ISBN 0 00 710072 8

Printed and bound in Great Britain by
Omnia Books Limited, Glasgow

Note

To protect the innocent – as well as the guilty – I have
changed and omitted some names. While I am pleased to
be able to tell the story of my life, I am only sorry that
I am still having to protect others.

Claire Beeken

Rosanna Greenstreet was born in 1963. She is a well-known national
newspaper and magazine journalist, specializing in celebrity inter-
views. She met Claire in 1994, when she interviewed her for a
magazine. The pair became friends, and Rosanna got involved with
the charity 'Caraline', taking on the role of Honorary Public Relations
& Media Manager. She is married with two daughters, and lives in
Hampshire. *My Body, My Enemy* is her first book.

This book is dedicated to my dear friend Caraline.
Caraline, I told you that while I was alive people would
speak your name. I have kept my promise.

Claire Beeken

Chapter one

The man who ruined my life was dressed as Father Christmas. We were sitting in the front room – Grandma, Mum, Dad, my big brother Michael, my new baby sister Lisa and I – when he walked in with his white beard, red suit and jolly 'Ho-Ho-Ho!'. I didn't realize who he was then, when I was three; and it's funny because now – when I watch the cine-film of Christmas 1973 – I still don't recognize him as my grandfather.

Granddad and Grandma were Dad's parents. They lived in the same street as us in Luton and we were a close family. Every Sunday they'd come to our house for dinner or we'd go to theirs. Michael and I totally adored them – there was no reason not to. Grandma was plump and always on a diet, but she loved her food too much. She had dark-grey hair and smoked in those days. Granddad smoked too. He liked Clan tobacco and walked round with his pipe in his mouth even when it wasn't lit. He had a hooked nose and, under the trilby he always wore, his pure-white hair was thinning. You could tell from his freckly skin that he'd once had bright-ginger hair. Michael and I favoured Granddad because he gave us sweets. So did our dog, Sabre, who was always sniffing his pockets. Granddad would fumble in his pocket, fish out his white handkerchief and the mints he always carried, dig a bit deeper and produce a Mars Bar for us each.

Mum and Dad were poor and really struggled when we were young. Dad worked across the road for a factory manufacturing ball-bearings. As soon as he came in at night, Mum would go out to her cleaning job at the same factory. Dad worked weekends as well, and on Sundays Mum would sit down with us kids to watch the afternoon movie on TV. I liked the old Elvis films and Mum loved anything starring Mario Lanza. Sometimes Mum would point out of the window and say, 'Look, there's Daddy.' We'd look up from the TV screen and there he'd be, waving from the roof of the factory wearing a big black coat with the name of the factory written on the back.

By the time my sister was three months old, money was the least of my parents' worries. Lisa developed serious breathing problems and at first it was thought she had cystic fibrosis. She was eventually diagnosed as a brittle asthmatic, and the doctors told my parents that she was unlikely to make it to her 18th birthday. Poor Mum and Dad were constantly in and out of hospital with Lisa, and my brother and I increasingly found ourselves at Grandma's for tea.

Grandma was a great cook – she made home-made doughnuts and did lovely roast potatoes. She used a lot of fat in her cooking and you'd be hit by the smell as you walked through the door. It was a typical old people's house: the carpet in the hall was an orange and brown pattern and in the front room stood Grandma's organ and a record-player in a long, old-fashioned cabinet. The records were Granddad's: he liked popular songs like 'Downtown' by Petula Clark and 'Stupid Cupid' by Connie Francis. The fireplace was almost completely obscured by a battery of family photographs, and on the wall opposite hung a rug with deer on it – I loved that rug. The stairs twisted up to the first bedroom which was Granddad's. It was a plain room with a wardrobe and two single beds. There were no books by his bed – he didn't read. Next door was the toilet with its creaky door and cold lino floor. It smelt of hospitals in there and sometimes, instead of toilet paper, there would be newspaper. In the bathroom there was a white enamel bath with lime-scale round the taps – but the house wasn't dirty, just old. My grandparents had separate rooms, and in Grandma's there was a double bed, a dressing table and a clock with a loud tick. By the bed there were always hardback books from the library by Catherine Cookson or Jean Plaidy, a pair of reading glasses with thick, milk-bottle lenses, and religious things like rosary beads and Mass cards. Lastly, there was a tiny boxroom which housed Grandma's big brown sewing machine with its fascinating pedals that I loved to press.

Grandma and Granddad's back garden was a sun-trap. You opened the kitchen door and stepped down two steps to the coal bunker, which we kids were just desperate to jump off. 'Get down!' the adults would yell. But we knew that if we were good Granddad would sit us up there. We weren't allowed to move a muscle until he lifted us back down, in case we hurt ourselves. A thin concrete path ran the length of the garden, and an apple tree grew on either side. Behind the trees stood the shed where Granddad did his carpentry. He used to work as a chippy and he made amazing pieces of furniture. He retired when I was seven and I remember his retirement 'do'. Dad has a picture of me at the party – I'm wearing a blue dotted dress and have two pink ribbons in my hair.

―――――――――

I am nine when he begins touching me. My parents have just started trusting me to make a pot of tea and I am keen to demonstrate my new skill to him. Grandma is out and I feel very grown-up as I stand in his kitchen waiting for the kettle to boil, carefully heaping the right amount of tea leaves into the cracked white pot and setting out mismatched cups and saucers. I am surprised when Granddad comes up behind me and clasps me to him. Even more so when he turns me around, bends down and kisses me hard on the lips. His close tobacco breath makes me gasp. 'I love you, I really love you,' he whispers as his freckly old hands work their way over my body like a pair of poisonous spiders. Trapped in the sun-bright kitchen, a swell of unease washes over me, and my innocence begins to dissolve.

It next happens when Grandma is away. I go round one afternoon to find Granddad watching a film. He loves old films and likes a bet, and you can guarantee he'll either be watching the horses or a black-and-white movie. I make the tea and sit next to him. 'I'd really like to take you to my boudoir,' he says softly. Boudoir? I don't know what a boudoir is. I am sitting there, turning the word over in my mind, when he says 'Kiss me.' I peck him on the cheek, as a little girl does. 'No, on the lips. Properly,' he insists, grabbing my face and forcing my lips to his. When he releases me I pipe up, 'What's a boudoir, Grand-dad?' 'I'll show you,' he says; and he does.

Chapter two

I think I might have dreamed what Granddad did, but the pain between my legs tells me it's real. He said he did it because he loves me, and I believe him. Granddad makes me feel special and, with all the attention on my sick little sister, I need to feel special. I know that Mum and Dad love me, but I am jealous of Lisa and her illness which takes up so much of their time. Granddad is showing me all this love and at first I want to hold on to it. 'Don't you love me today, Granddad?' I say when he doesn't touch me.

What he does to me hurts, but I switch my mind to other things: meadows, flowers, whole episodes of *Coronation Street*. I lie there re-enacting the antics of Jack and Vera Duckworth and Hilda Ogden in my head, while the white-faced alarm clock by my grandfather's bed ticks away my childhood. Afterwards I feel like a zombie. I eat the Mars Bar he always gives me and walk home in a daze – alone if it is daylight, under grandfatherly escort if it is dark.

'Why are you always kissing Claire, Granddad?'

asks my cousin. We are sitting watching television while the rest of the family are outside. Granddad keeps coming back indoors, leaning over the back of the settee and sticking soggy kisses on my forehead. Granddad doesn't answer the question, but looks down at me and winks. I feel awkward in the spotlight of my grandfather's attention, and wish I could fall between the settee cushions like a lost penny.

I love Granddad, but what he's doing doesn't feel right and I need to know if it is normal. 'What does your Granddad do with you?' I quiz a girl in my class at school. 'Oh, he takes me to the park and buys me ice cream and we have fun,' she breezes. 'Does he cuddle you?' I ask. 'Yes, he cuddles me,' says my classmate. 'What else does he do?' I probe. 'Nothing, why?' she says. 'No reason,' I reply, changing the subject quickly.

I start being frightened to go to my grandparents' house on my own. Grandma goes away a lot – to her sister's or her son's, and once to see her brother in Canada for a six-week holiday. 'Why don't you go down and see Granddad?' Mum would say. 'You know you're his favourite.' I'd feel the familiar scream rise up inside me: 'But I don't want to be Granddad's favourite. It doesn't make me feel good. I don't feel right being Granddad's favourite.' But my pain never slips out. Instead it moulders away in my head. I begin to develop searing migraines, and lie clutching my head while a rat seems to gnaw inside my skull. I cry a lot too, but never in front of anyone. I huddle up in my bed under the window, and through my tears I pray to God to take me away. I am always saying sorry to Him because I think I must be really bad. Why else does He let it keep happening to me? Why else am I being punished?

My 10th birthday is in April, and around this time my headaches become more frequent. I am also finding it difficult to eat – I can't shake the feeling that a bad thing will happen to me if I put something in my mouth. Mum and Dad don't notice at first, probably because I've been a difficult eater since the day I was born. During my first few months I had a bad chest and couldn't eat and breathe at the same time; I had to be fed like a little chick, every hour, 24 hours a day. The cine-film of my christening shows me looking like a war baby in a television news report.

I grow to be a faddy eater and particularly loathe school dinners, which annoys the dinner lady, Mrs Bacon. Her real name is Mrs something else but for some reason I've got it into my head that she's called Mrs 'Bacon'. One day, when I am six, she insists I stay behind to eat the dinner which, as usual, I have barely touched. The other children scatter to the playground, and I am left in the dining hall listening to their distant shouts. Mrs Bacon sits over me in her sickly-patterned overall and makes me eat. 'I'm going to be ill if you make me eat any more,' I say, staring into my bowl of semolina. 'You've got to eat it,' she insists. I take another mouthful and my body gives a tremendous heave. Out fly the cabbage, the mash, the meat and the semolina with its little dollop of pink jam – all over the blue Formica tabletop and onto the floor. Mrs Bacon looks horrified, and shoos me off to the medical room as fast as she can. With a feeling of relief, I leave her to cover my dinner with the powdery disinfectant that always lies like a sand-dune after somebody has been sick.

As I get older, I refuse to eat anything resembling an animal or fish. I'll happily tuck into sausages, beefburgers and fish-fingers but won't touch sliced ham, roast beef or lamb. I eat chicken – but not the skin – and for some reason I never eat sandwiches unless they've been made by me or my mum.

Mum and Dad have always taken it for granted that I am a fussy, skinny kid, but when I get even fussier and skinnier during the autumn of 1980, they start to worry. After I've been off school for several days with a migraine and unable to manage any food at all, Mum takes me to the doctor. My plummeting weight and excruciating headaches point to meningitis, and I am whisked into the Children's Annexe of Luton and Dunstable Hospital for tests.

At first they put me in a room on my own and I hate it: I pick at the awful food and am bored because I'm not allowed out of bed. Worst of all I am missing school. I hate school too, but I've been cast as the Virgin Mary in the school Christmas play. Grandma gave me a painted statue of the Virgin which I keep on the sill in my bedroom and carefully lift down onto my bed to dust. She is my pride and joy, and it has been my dream to play Mary since I was in the Infants. Rehearsals for the play have started, and I am worried that my understudy will get her hands on my part while I'm in hospital. Her name is Fleur: 'It's French for flower, you know,' she says snottily.

After a couple of days, Dad brings in the small black-and-white TV we take on camping holidays. I am lying in bed watching the end of *Tiswas* when a nurse comes in. She sits down and says she'll read me a story from *Black Beauty* – I love *Black Beauty*, and like to pretend that I am Jenny. I settle down to listen to the story, but the nurse says, 'You're going to have a lumbar puncture this afternoon.' 'Is it going to hurt?' I ask. 'A little bit,' she says, looking away and launching into the story. I can tell by her face that she's lying.

———

The painful room is through the double doors at the far end of the ward. Where blood tests are taken and injections given, it contains a bed and a screen and looks out over the hospital garden. A doctor and four nurses fill the room, and although I can't see any needles, I can smell them. 'Hop up on the bed, Claire, and turn over onto your front,' the doctor says from behind his white mask. Rigid with fear I lie down on the bed. The nurses close ranks around me and arrange my body for the procedure. I am wearing a paper gown which ties up at the back, and no knickers, and my bottom lies cold and exposed. Wham! – in goes the injection. I shriek with shock and kick out at the nurses. They press down on my back and hold my legs and arms. 'If you let us do it, it will be over very quickly,' says one of the nurses. After an interval I hear him instruct the nurse 'And again!' Bam! – in goes another injection. I thrash like a harpooned seal, and scream and scream until the sedative takes effect and there's no scream left. Then they turn me onto my side and insert the biggest needle of all into my spine to extract fluid from around my brain, and I don't feel a thing.

Later, bent with pain from the lumbar puncture and still getting headaches, I am dosed with pain-killers and can't face the hospital food. Over the next few days the nurses keep pestering me to eat, which I find irritating. 'What's the big deal?' I say. 'I'm not hungry.' Then the threats start. 'If you don't start to eat, Claire, we're going to have to feed you through a drip.' They transfer me to the General Ward where, too weak to walk from lack of food, I lie watching the girl in the bed opposite. She has lots of aunts and is surrounded by boxes and boxes of chocolates they've brought in for her. I love sweets, and envy her as she absent-mindedly pops them into her mouth. She catches me staring and asks if I'd like a chocolate. 'No, thank you,' I say, rather surprised at the feeling of superiority it gives me.

I haven't eaten for three or four days when the big black matron settles herself on my bed with a bowl of Weetabix. She's smothered the cereal with sugar and poured on loads of milk – I loathe milk. 'The doctor says you have to eat this, Claire,' she says, thrusting the bowl under my nose. 'I don't want it,' I protest. 'I'm not hungry'. 'You've got to eat it, Claire,' she repeats. 'No, no, no,' I insist. 'I can't!' With that she holds my nose, my mouth springs open and in goes the spoon: it rattles against my teeth as matron tips the soggy mess down my throat. She repeats the process a couple of times and then lets me up for air. 'If you don't want me to do it, you've got to feed yourself,' she says. Burning with humiliation, I eat the rest unaided.

I am scared of meal-times after that. Each morning I dread the rumble of the steel trolley bearing down on me with its unwanted load of Weetabix,

cornflakes, puffed wheat and piles of white bread
and butter. I hear the metal jugs of milk rattle and
catch the nauseating smell of Ready Brek as it wafts
across the ward. I'm not going to risk another force-
feeding so I ask for Weetabix, and fling most of it
into the cupboard by my bed.

Matron gets wise to my trick and makes me sit
at the table in the centre of the ward with the other
patients. 'I've got to go to the toilet,' I say to the
chocolate girl one dinner-time and leg it down the
ward to the toilets next to the painful room. I bolt
the cubicle door and pray: 'Dear Lord Jesus Christ,
please don't let them know I'm in here. Please don't
let them look for me. I can't eat. Don't let them find
me. I promise I'll eat tomorrow.' There is an almighty
bang on the door. Matron! 'Claire, open this door. If
you don't, we'll come in and get you!' Sheepishly, I
unlock the door and come out. Matron propels me to
the table, but I howl and scream and will not eat.

'I'm going to pull the wool over your eyes,' I
think to myself when the consultant is on his rounds
next day. 'Hello, Claire. How are you this morning?'
he asks. 'Fine, really well,' I say brightly. 'I'm ready
to go home.' 'You're not eating much, Claire,' he
says, casting his eye over the chart at the bottom of
my bed. 'It's the food in here,' I say, with all the conviction I can muster. 'Mum cooks lovely food; I'll eat
loads when I get home.' 'Okay,' says the doctor. 'You
can go home.' I can't believe it. 'Yes!' I think. 'I'm
going to be Mary!'

Mum and Dad come to collect me the following
morning. They've brought my brown polo-neck
jumper and matching checked skirt for me to wear
and, as Mum zips up the skirt, it spins round like a

hoop on a stick. I can see by Mum's face that she isn't happy. Poor Mum and Dad; I've been in hospital for three weeks and meningitis has been ruled out; but I'm still having headaches and not eating properly. Worry puckers their faces as they exchange glances and go to speak to Matron, and I am convinced they aren't going to take me home. 'That's it, I'm off!' I think, starting for the exit, but I am so weak and full of painkillers that I collapse and throw up.

The consultant is called and I barely notice him slip the intravenous drip into the vein in the back of my hand. But half an hour afterwards I begin to feel much, much better. I spend a week rigged up to the drip and Granddad continues to visit me most afternoons. He sits on the bed, asks how I am and gives me a Mars Bar. 'Thank you,' I say politely, laying it to one side, safe in the knowledge that he won't touch me because there are other people around.

One afternoon I actually feel like eating something, but I don't want his Mars Bar. 'I'm hungry,' I say to Granddad. Looking pleased, he rushes off to tell a nurse. She comes over with the tea trolley. 'I want that,' I say, pointing to a little iced chocolate cake with a diamond jelly in the centre. As I bite into it the nurse says, 'You know, if you eat we'll take this drip down and you'll be able to go home.' 'And then I can be Mary,' I think to myself. So I eat, and 48 hours later I am home.

The whole family turns out to see me in the Christmas play. 'Your daughter has the voice of an angel,' says somebody else's mother to my parents. Mum tells me afterwards that Granddad cried.

Chapter three

'If someone hits you, you hit them back,' Dad says when I come home from school in tears. I am the loner whom everybody picks on. A girl in my class keeps threatening to beat me up and, after Mum buys me a new coat, the bully dumps it in the bin. Other kids say I am ugly and that I smell, and because I'm so skinny they call me 'Skeletal', 'Stick Insect' and 'Xylophone'.

I still feel funny about food and am not eating normally. I never eat breakfast. If I go home from school for dinner Mum gives me soup or a sandwich which I sometimes eat, sometimes not. When I take in a packed lunch, I throw the sandwiches away and stuff myself with sweets instead. Mum would have killed me if she'd known, but because I usually manage my tea she doesn't realize I'm not eating properly.

After a while I stop telling Mum and Dad that I'm being picked on – they've enough to worry about with Lisa, and what is happening to me at school isn't half as bad as what happens to me at Granddad's.

At the age of 11, I start at Lealands High. Mum says, 'Sit with people you don't know, so you make more friends.' But I don't. I sit next to Yvonne whom I know from junior school. Yvonne is bullied too because she has no hair. She is having chemotherapy for leukaemia and has to wear a scarf, and people pull it off to make her cry.

'When you are older and you've got a job, you'll wish you were back at school,' Dad says. 'Bet you a million pounds I won't,' I reply. I hate everything about school with two exceptions – dance and music. Our dance and music teacher is a blonde lady called Mrs Patterson. She's rather plump but she can dance, and is a real tra-la-laaaa singer. She knows how to put a show together and always gives me lead parts. 'I'm the gypsy – the acid queen,' I mime along to Tina Turner's soundtrack. We are doing *Orpheus and the Underworld* using the music from the films *Tommy* and *Grease*. With my face painted silver, a glitter disco dress and my head swathed in snakes, I am the Acid Queen and Ian Carrington is the Devil. Mrs Patterson always pairs me off with Ian who is the best boy dancer. I do a back-flip over him and then we launch into 'You're The One That I Want'.

When I am singing and dancing I feel different – I let go of my problems and am light and free. I look forward to Tuesdays and Thursdays when we have dance and music, and always sneak off games and go to the dance room instead. 'Patterson-lover' the other kids call me, but I don't care. I only once refuse Mrs Patterson. She wants me to play a belly-dancer in a pair of see-through net trousers over red knickers and a little bra-top. It is like being in your underwear and there is no way I'm doing it because it shows my body, and I know Granddad will be coming to watch.

'Mum, you know Granddad?' I say one day when I am 12 and desperately wanting to tell. 'Yes?' she replies. But the words wedge in my throat – what if she doesn't believe me, what if I split up the family? I change the subject and swallow my terrible secret. As it festers inside, my behaviour worsens. I am either extremely high or extremely low. When I come home from school I often go upstairs to my bedroom and shut the door. I lie there for a good hour listening to my stereo before I can bring myself to speak to anyone. I love my family, but one of them is hurting me.

I have to share my bedroom with Lisa. We have Holly Hobbie wallpaper and matching duvets – Lisa is allergic to sheets and blankets. There are two white fitted cupboards along one wall with a dressing table in the middle. On it I keep my jewellery box which plays *Swan Lake* when you open it, and a bottle of 'Rose' perfume that I bought from the Avon lady. Lisa is hard to share a room with because when she isn't having an asthma attack she is being neurotic. Before she can go to sleep she has to touch the light switch over and over again, and say 'Goodnight, God bless, sweet dreams' to me 50 times. But I pay her back with my own catalogue of nocturnal twitches.

Sometimes, when I'm asleep, my eyes open. I go to bed early one night and Lisa comes in, thinks I am awake and starts talking to me. My subconscious may be keeping watch for the enemy, but I am fast asleep. Poor Lisa runs screaming down the stairs to Mum, thinking I am dead.

My sleep-walking frightens the hell out of Lisa too. She wakes to find me shouting, pulling the curtains and trying to climb out of the window. Another night she has one of her nosebleeds and, thinking I am awake, asks me to get her some loo paper. I go downstairs to the bathroom and come back with a hairbrush. 'What good's that going to do?' she says, packing me off downstairs again. Apparently, I wrench the toilet-roll off its holder, go into Mum and Dad's bedroom, turn on the light, lob the loo roll at Dad's head and go back to bed. I am asleep the entire time.

'Play with me, Claire,' Lisa is always moaning. I don't want to, but sometimes Mum makes me. We play *The Wizard of Oz*, but I always make sure that I am Dorothy, and Lisa is the Witch. As we grow older we have more in common, and when I am 13 and she is 9 we are both *Fame* mad – I have a *Fame* T-shirt and a *Fame* dance outfit – and love Thursday nights because *Fame* is on TV. I am finding it harder and harder to stomach my evening meal and, to Mum and Dad's annoyance, pick at my food and push it round the plate; but on Thursdays I eat everything. I am always extra-hungry because I've had dance at school and then done my paper-round which means a lot of uphill walking. Mum cooks burgers and ravioli or a curry – I love her curries – and then she goes late-night shopping, leaving Lisa and me scoffing toffees in front of *Fame*.

'Karen Carpenter has died from the effects of anorexia,' it says on the News on 4 February 1983. They show a video clip of her singing 'Mr Postman' while she flies around on the elephants at Disneyland. 'What was the matter with her, Dad?' I ask. I like The Carpenters: when I was little I used to stand on Dad's toes and we'd dance around to their music. 'She bleedin' starved herself to death, didn't she! Silly girl, throwing all that away,' he says. I don't understand it. I've never heard of anorexia, and my poor father never dreams that it is a word that will become all too familiar.

Everybody calls me 'Stick Insect' and takes the pee out of me, but I don't think I am as thin as a girl in my class called Kate; now, she is disgustingly thin! 'You're very thin, Kate,' I say. 'You're a lot skinnier than me,' she protests. 'I'm not,' I say, getting annoyed. We end up in some almighty rows. When we are in a childcare lesson, we get out the scales to settle it once and for all. I am gutted, absolutely gutted – she weighs 7 stone, I weigh $6\frac{1}{2}$. I really thought I was bigger than her. It makes me so angry to be constantly teased about my weight, but it never crosses my mind that if I eat more I'll get bigger.

———————————

I might be skinny but inside I boil with an aggression that puts the fear of God into my fellow cadets in the Air Training Corps. My brother Michael is in the ATC first and I keep badgering his squadron leader to let me join. 'Girls put up wallpaper and paint pretty patterns. They can't be in the ATC,' scoff Michael and his friend Glyn, who are both in Icknield Squadron.

But I want to do athletics and shoot with guns and go on weekend camps like the boys. When I am 14 the squadron leader relents and lets me enrol; and the boys in the squadron hate it.

'Get over here!' the squadron leader yells, and I love it. I try really hard not to be girly; I practise shooting with a 303 rifle until my shoulder is purple with bruises, and scrap with the best of them. I adore my airforce blue uniform – the thick serge trousers, the big jumper with patches, the beret with its badge and, best of all, the huge pair of Doc Marten boots with steel toe-caps.

We are on night exercise near Aylesbury and have been split into two teams. My team has to find the bomb the enemy has planted and bring it back to camp. The squadron leader blindfolds us and drives us round and round in a van until we don't have a clue where we are. Then he unties our blindfolds and dumps us in a field. It's pitch-black and we have a great time diving on haystacks thinking they are the enemy. And then I spot a boy we call 'Mong' who is on the other team. Leaving my team behind I charge through the bushes, grab his legs, and throw him to the ground. Before he can scramble up, I sit on him. 'Where's the bomb? Where's the bomb?' I shout, laying into the enemy with my fists. 'Please don't hurt me, please don't hurt me!' the poor bloke begs. I am the lightest in the squadron, but I am on a mission and 'Mong' doesn't stand a chance. After that, all the boys want me in their team, otherwise I end up half-killing them!

When I'm not exorcising my anger in the ATC, or pushing myself through punishing dance routines to ease my pain, I spend hours and hours playing with my pets. I prefer them to people – animals don't hurt you.

Our house is a regular zoo. After Sabre dies, we get another Alsation called Drummer, and have three fish – Freddie, Goldie and Rainbow, so-called because she has red lips, and four rabbits which I name Bramble, Holly, Smoky and Thumper. We start off with Bramble and Holly, and we kids buy Smoky for Mum and then Thumper for Dad one Father's Day. With each new addition our long-suffering father extends the existing hutch upwards.

Out shopping one Saturday I fall in love with a guinea-pig in the pet shop. I know Dad won't be pleased when I come home with yet another pet, but I want this guinea-pig badly. He looks just like a ginger scrubbing brush and I call him Fibre. I pay £3 for him, and carry him home in a cardboard box. Well, Dad goes spare! There is no room to add another floor to the high-rise hutch and he says I have to take Fibre back to the shop. But good old Granddad saves the day. He offers to make Fibre a hutch but says I have to help him. Grandma says if I go down one night after school she'll do me tea. I know what I'm letting myself in for, but I want to keep my guinea-pig so much that I agree.

It's hot, and I'm wearing a white, short-sleeved shirt tucked into my school skirt. It is a long pencil skirt, and I look like a pencil – I really do. I'm in a stinking mood all day, and can't concentrate in lessons because my mind keeps turning to what's going to happen later. I walk out of the school gates towards Grandma and Granddad's feeling sick, but the thought of Fibre going back to the pet shop propels me along. 'Hello,' says Grandma when I walk into the kitchen. 'Granddad's in the shed.'

The shed is really a garage which Granddad has turned into a workshop. It is made of grey corrugated metal and has two big windows which face the house but are obscured by the apple trees. As I walk towards the shed, hard little windfalls slide under my shoes and make me lose my footing. The entrance is round the side, and as I walk through the open door, I am met by the smell of sawdust, oily rags and Granddad's pipe. I can see that the double garage doors at the back of the building are blocked by shelves laden with tools and rusty tins oozing sticky stuff. Years later, when I see the film *Nightmare on Elm Street*, Freddy Kreuger's den reminds me of that shed. 'Hello, darlin',' grins Granddad, looking up from the most beautiful hutch I've ever seen. He's left a few nails for me to knock in, and I dutifully go over and hammer them in. Then, without a word, he shoots the bolt on the shed door – and what I dread most happens.

Afterwards, when I go back into the house, I can't manage the egg and chips that Grandma has cooked for me. I demolish the Mars Bar which Granddad gives me though. I always eat his Mars Bars in a particular way. I unwrap the top half and press my thumb down on the chocolate coating until it cracks and the soft centre starts to ooze out. I like to see the chocolate mash between my fingers. Then I start to pull bits off it and stuff them into my mouth as fast as I can. As I force each piece down my gullet, my hand is poised at my lips with the next bit. Sometimes I eat so quickly that I swallow pieces of wrapper. I don't enjoy the chocolate, I don't taste it; I just eat until it is gone, and so fast that I often feel sick. It is a ritual – when the Mars is finished, the bad thing is over.

Chapter four

'Have you got hair?' I ask Yvonne. 'You know I haven't,' she laughs, tugging at her blue and white dotted scarf. 'No, not on your head,' I say, mouthing 'down there.' 'No,' she says, looking bemused. 'God,' I think to myself, 'I'm even more ugly than I thought.'

Most of the girls in my class start their periods in our second year at Lealands; mine don't come until much later. 'You wait till you get breasts, you wait till your periods come; then you'll be a real woman,' Granddad keeps saying, and I am terrified. If this is happening to me now, when I don't have periods or breasts, what is going to happen to me when I do?

I start my periods at the end of the summer term when I am fourteen; and then, when I am on holiday in Blackpool with Mum, Dad and Lisa, my breasts grow – literally overnight. We are staying in a self-catering apartment and Lisa and I are sharing a bed. My little bumps are agony whichever way I lie, and my arms don't know where to put themselves. Next morning I take off my nightdress to find that my molehills have turned into mountains. I am astonished – and ashamed.

I hate my boobs because he likes to touch them, and my periods because they excite him. My body feels infected and dirty, and when I catch sight of myself in the mirror, I am disgusted by it. My classmates are right – I am ugly and I probably do smell. I hate my body, hate my life and find myself looking at other boys and girls and wishing I could be them instead of me. God forgive me, I even wish I had cancer like Yvonne.

Yvonne has been off school for ages, and I visit her at home. She is really into the Royal Family, and shows me her scrapbook filled with pictures of the Prince and Princess of Wales's wedding and baby Prince William. The last time I see Yvonne she has a patch over her eye, and talks a lot about a bone marrow transplant. I don't really understand what she means, and it is a shock when Mum tells me one dinner-time that Yvonne is in a coma. 'Will she wake up?' I ask. 'Nobody knows, love,' says Mum, and I cry.

In December, a girl comes flying down the school corridor shouting 'Yvonne's dead!'. I want to go home and ask Mrs Patterson to let me off choir practice, but she won't. I have to stand there and sing, my grief spilling onto the wooden floor. On the day of the funeral, I am in a real state. As Yvonne's coffin is lowered into the ground, I weep and weep. 'God's got to get his angels from somewhere, Claire,' says Yvonne's auntie, putting her arms around me. She isn't to know that part of me is crying because I want to be the one who is dead.

With my best friend gone, I hate school even more, and in June 1985 I am pleased to have three

weeks off, doing work experience at British Home
Stores. Each day I go into town on the bus, and work
from 8.45 a.m. to 5.45 p.m. I love it. I am proud of my
uniform – the pale-blue blouse and dark-blue A-line
pinafore with its special loop for my locker key. I like
the other staff who treat me like one of them, and not
like a schoolgirl. Best of all, Mr Warner, the manager,
says that if I am any good he'll consider me for a Saturday job.

I work in all the departments – lighting, children,
fashions, menswear, toys, the lot. When deliveries
come I collect them from the stock room and sort
them out. I tidy, count stock and fill out the DAS –
the daily alteration sheet. I am too young to work on
the till, but if there is a queue I jump up and wrap for
the cashier.

'You need fattening up,' says Sheila, who works on
one of the tills. She is an older lady and I am gobs-
macked by her rings – three or four big gold ones, with
diamonds, on each finger! She calls me 'Little Love',
'Skinny Lizzy' and 'Rag Doll Annie' and she's always
saying, 'Let's go and have a nice cream cake.' It becomes a joke between us. She gives me sweets, and at
tea break she sits next to me in the canteen and tries to
tempt me with her cream cake. I don't like cream and I
won't eat the cake, but I love Sheila to bits.

The canteen is upstairs and has a pool table and a
table-tennis table, comfy seats and the sort of carpet
that would hurt your feet if you didn't have shoes on.
I eat well during those three weeks. I feel happy and
comfortable and the canteen food is lovely. A book of
meal vouchers costs staff £1.50 each week, but because I am on work experience I get mine free: a
white main meal ticket and two pink tea-break ones

every day. In the morning you can help yourself to tea, coffee, orange or lemon, and there are warm rolls from the bakery across the road. The canteen cook fills them with cheese – the smell drifts down to the shop floor, and I look forward to my morning break. Dinner is home-made lasagne or steak and kidney pie with vegetables, and a hot pudding like jam roly-poly and custard. I tell Mum not to do me tea because I am eating so much at work.

At the end of my work experience Mrs Sansom, the personnel manageress, calls me into her office. 'We'd like to offer you four hours' work every Saturday,' she says; and I am so pleased. My hours are 10 a.m. till 2 p.m. and my wages are £5.53 a day. With my bus fare at 55p each way I am left with a grand total of £4.43 – but I think it's a fortune. Soon after, the summer holidays begin, and a vacancy comes up for a Saturday job with more hours. I am thrilled when Mrs Sansom gives it to me and increases my money to £10.37.

⸻

That summer, when I'm not working at BHS, I spend my days at Alka Patel's house. I've known Alka since infant school, but after Yvonne dies we hang around together. Alka is pretty, and can put on liquid eyeliner perfectly – being Indian she's worn make-up since she was little. Her family are so different – Alka has to help with the cooking and cleaning before she's allowed out.

I watch Alka making chapattis. Her little flour-covered fingers coax the doughy mixture into perfect circles: she makes it look easy and I ask if I can have a go. Well I huff and puff over this chapatti, and the more I labour the more leaden and lumpy it becomes. 'It looks like the map of India!' I announce when I've finished, and Alka and her mother laugh their heads off.

I am the only English girl Alka's mother likes because she thinks I'm polite – she doesn't realize what we get up to when she goes out. Once we get into a play fight with a couple of squeezy bottles of tomato ketchup. Up and down the street we dash, squirting each other's bare legs red, and my sister from head to toe!

Back at school after the summer holidays, despair descends. I am still being bullied at school and abused at home. When I know I have to go to Granddad's house after a day of bullying, I feel absolutely desperate. The abuse seems to affect me more now that I am 15. It had always felt wrong; but now we are doing reproduction in biology, I know it's wrong. It isn't the sort of thing a grandfather is supposed to do to his granddaughter, and I begin to think that if Granddad stops perhaps I'll feel better. I make up my mind to say something next time I see him.

It is a Sunday afternoon when he comes round. I am sitting at the kitchen table pondering over my essay which is called 'Why I would make a good head girl'. Whoever writes the best essay becomes the next head girl, and I really want to show my parents that I can do something. Michael and Lisa study hard but I don't, and Mum and Dad always say that I don't try. 'You won't pass, Claire,' they said when I asked them to pay for me to do English 'O' level. Even my English teacher said, 'I don't know why you are bothering.

You're not going to be able to do it.' Everyone thinks I am incapable; but I'm insisting on doing it, and paying to take the exam with my paper-round money.

Mum and Dad are getting ready to take the dog for a walk when Granddad turns up. My essay has to be in on Monday morning and I really want to do a good job. 'Oh, no!' I think to myself. 'If they go out, he's going to start on me and I won't get my essay done.' I begin to get stroppy, trying to start an argument in the hope that it might stop my parents going out. Dad ends up slapping my face, but they go out anyway.

I begin to write my essay, but can't concentrate because I can feel Granddad all around me. 'Give me a hug,' he says. I put down the pen, stand up and give him as loose a hug as I can. I go to sit down, but he clings on like an old mollusc. 'I love you, I love you,' he mutters, rubbing my boobs. 'Stop; just stop!' I say, my heart pounding and my voice rising. 'I don't like what you're doing!' There, I've said it. His hands fall away from my breasts and tears fly from his eyes. He stumbles from the kitchen into the front room where he crumples into a pathetic heap. I follow and find him sobbing into his handkerchief, 'I'm sorry, I'm so sorry darlin'. I just love you.' I feel really bad about upsetting him and start to cry too. 'I'm sorry too,' I weep, 'but you love me in the wrong way.' He wipes his eyes and is gone before Mum and Dad get home, but my essay never gets written.

———————————

We have some right laughs, Lisa Duxbury and I. She has a Saturday job at British Home Stores too and, being the same age, we've become friends. In the early

summer of 1986 we are both looking forward to getting our exams out of the way and leaving school for
good. She's at Icknield High, but we meet up in the
town centre after school.

One day we are messing about in Boots on one of
those electronic machines that print out your weight.
We have great fun jumping on and off the scales and
ripping off the print-outs. I don't even bother to look
at the slip of paper, just stuff it in my skirt pocket.
Later, when I'm polishing my ATC boots on a piece
of newspaper by the back door, I remember the
print-out. 'I wonder what my weight is,' I think,
pulling it out of my pocket. 8 stone 2. 'Wouldn't it
be good if it said 8 stone?' says a little voice in my
head, and I agree.

'I know,' I think to myself, 'I'll have an apple for
breakfast, an orange for lunch and a banana for tea.' I
tell Mum what I'm going to do and she just gives me
a look as if to say, 'Faddy!'

Three days later the print-out says 7 stone 13. 'It
works!' I say to myself. Up pipes the little voice,
'Wouldn't it be good if it said 7 stone 10?' 'Mmm, that
sounds good,' I think.

'You've got to eat more than an apple, an orange
and a banana,' Mum says, having no nonsense. 'I
dunno,' I think, inspecting myself in the mirror, 'the
scales say I'm losing weight but I think I'm getting
bigger.' Down at Boots again the slip says 7 stone 10,
but the number isn't magic any more and the voice
insists, 'Wouldn't it be good if it said 7 stone 7?'

'You don't need to lose any more weight,' says
Mum, putting her foot down. 'You've got to eat.'
'Okay,' I say – anything for a quiet life. It's June and
I've left school early to start working full-time at

British Home Stores, so it's easy to tell Mum that I'm eating my main meal in the canteen.

When Lisa Duxbury comes to work on a Saturday, she says, 'Claire, you're only eating an apple, an orange and a banana and you're looking really thin.' 'Don't be stupid,' I say. 'I'm *fat*.'

'Everyone's stopping for a break, Claire. I think you should too,' says Mrs Sansom. We are doing a Sunday stock-take and I've been asked to dress a set of mannequins – everyone says I've a flair for it. I've chosen emerald green and royal blue clothes, and am fiddling about with beads and bangles and having a great time. 'Okay, Mrs Sansom, let me just finish this.' 'You can finish it in a minute, Claire.' 'Yeah, but I just want...' 'You can do that in a minute. Please go up to the canteen and have something to eat.' The rest of the staff are tucking in to their roast dinners but I just have a glass of lemon. My stomach is grinding round and round like a washing machine. I am running on empty, but I'm high on an overwhelming feeling of control. I take agitated little sips with one eye on my watch: I want the lunch-break to end so that I can get back to being creative.

'What did you eat at work today, Claire?' asks Mum when she picks me up in the car. 'Chicken, roast potatoes, vegetables,' I say, automatically. 'Liar!' she spits. 'Mrs Sansom rang to tell me you haven't eaten a thing all day. All you've had are a couple of drinks, and she said other staff have been going up to her and saying that you haven't been eating.' 'I have, Mum, they just haven't seen me,' I protest weakly. 'Don't lie to me,' she screams. 'What are you trying to do; kill yourself? When you get home you're not doing anything until you've had something to eat.' 'Oh my God, I can't!' I think, shaky with panic and anger. 'How dare Mrs Sansom ring Mum up! How dare she!'

'Go and sit in the garden and I'll bring you out something,' says Mum. I sink into a deckchair at the far end of the garden and watch Mum walk towards me with a tray and a determined look on her face. 'They're trying to make you fat,' whispers the voice in my head as I gaze in horror at the two thick slices of freshly cut bread, the slab of butter and tub of cream cheese. To me they are huge doorsteps, if not whole loaves, and the sight of the cream cheese makes me want to retch. I can't eat it. It'll fill my emptiness and I won't feel light any more. I'll never reach 7 stone 4. Tears pour from my eyes as I beg my mother not to make me eat. Fear flickers across her face, and it makes her angry. 'You're not bloody moving until you've eaten that!' she yells, adding, 'I rang your granddad up this afternoon and told him about you and you broke his heart.' Then I howl.

A few days later I nip into Boots and weigh myself again – 7 stone 4. 'Wow!' I think to myself. 'I can't stop this now; I want to get to 7. I want to be 7 stone.' I have something that is mine, but it's a game that people keep trying to take away from me and I'm not going to let them. Manipulation becomes my middle name. 'I *am* eating,' I lie to Mrs Sansom. 'I'm just going to lose a few pounds and then I'll stop,' I convince my friend Lisa, adding 'but don't tell Mum; she doesn't understand.' I start taking a sandwich with me to work. I make sure people see me put it in the fridge at work and take it out again at dinner-time. Then I go out for my dinner hour, and bin the sandwich in the town centre.

I buy a calorie-counting book which gives the calories in every sort of food you can think of, and a set of bathroom scales. Stupid with worry, my parents think I'm going to work out a sensible diet with the book and use the scales to maintain my weight. And I let them believe it.

'Nimble bread – 55 calories a slice.' I read the calorie book like a bible every night. 'Weight Watchers soup, minestrone – 53 calories per can; apple – 50 calories; banana – a whopping 95 calories!' The banana will have to go! By the time I get down to 7 stone, my periods have stopped and Mum is at the end of her tether. 'Right,' she says. 'If you're eating at work, that's fine; but you're going to have something in front of me each night.' There are tears, rows and screaming matches. 'Don't be so bloody stupid, Claire. Are you trying to kill yourself? Think of all the starving children in Africa!' Mum and Dad rant and rave. On and on at me they go until things get so bad, I give in.

Because I am so thin, I gain weight on just one meal a day. The game appears to be over, but inside I am still trying to outwit the enemy. Destructive thoughts race about my head. 'Look at that disgusting fat body. I'm too big. I take up too much space. I shouldn't have had that. I've got to be small.'

Chapter five

I am working in the children's department when Kim Speight comes in for her interview. She's wearing an electric-blue skirt, a leather jacket and carrying a fold-up umbrella under her arm. Her long brown hair has been tonged at the back into two fat sausages which bounce up and down as she walks upstairs to the office. 'Snooty cow,' I say to myself, peering at her from behind a rack.

'I dunno,' I think when Kim starts a week later. 'Maybe she isn't so snooty, and at least she's someone my own age.' So when I bump into her in the stock room, I say hello and we get chatting. The following week, BHS holds a shopping evening for staff and their families. Mum can't make it, so Kim asks me to go with her and her mum. I go back to Kim's house after work and her mum is really nice: she cooks sausages and jacket potatoes for tea, which are lovely. We have a real giggle at the shopping evening and go on to become inseparable: Sheila calls us the terrible twins.

I still see Lisa Duxbury, but not as often because

she's given up her Saturday job and is studying at college to be a hotel receptionist. Kim and I start going clubbing together and spend hours in her bedroom trying on clothes. Her parents live apart, and sometimes we go round to her dad's for tea. Often he gets us a Chinese takeaway and he always has bowls of sweets and fun-size chocolate bars dotted around the house. Kim stuffs herself – Kim is skinny; and somehow it seems okay if I do the same. I rush at the sweets, excited by the forbidden. 'This is bad; you're bad,' says the little voice as I chew and swallow and, afterwards, I hate myself.

'What does your waist measure, Kim?' I ask, eyeing her with envy. She's bought the most beautiful royal-blue pleated skirt from Dorothy Perkins and her waist looks tiny. I've got the same skirt, but it isn't as nice on me because my waist is bigger than Kim's. 'Twenty-two inches,' she says. And with those three little words, the game cranks back to life. 'Right,' I say to myself, 'I'm going on a diet.' The delicate balance that has kept me at a steady $7^1/_2$ stone tips, and sends me helter-skelter into the land of fun-house mirrors where thin is fat and food is greed, and the calorie book rules okay.

'Do you girls want a Chinese?' asks Kim's dad, one night after work. 'Yes please,' says Kim. 'No thanks,' I say. 'Are you sure?' Kim asks. 'You haven't eaten much today.' 'I'm alright, I'm just not hungry,' I lie. Kim chooses what I usually have – chicken fried rice, curry sauce and chips – and I want it so much. I watch her eat and, smelling it, I can almost taste it. I am hungry and cold and my body is growling in protest. I touch my tummy, but it isn't there and I am temporarily sated by a sense of superiority. Later Kim and I go upstairs to change to go out. 'Bloody hell,' says Kim as I undress. 'Look at your stomach – it's gone right in!'

At work my uniform flops off me. 'Wow! My legs have got longer and my bum's disappeared!' I think to myself as I run my hand down my skirt. 'What an achievement!' If someone offers me a sweet I say, 'No thank you.'

There are rows at home and people notice at work. I am summoned to Mrs Sansom's office where she and Mr Warner tell me that if I don't eat properly, my parents will be informed and I'll be suspended. My job entails running up and down ladders and lifting things, and it seems I am a danger in the workplace. I run crying to Kim. 'But Claire,' she says, 'you know you're not eating.' The voice in my head is insistent: 'They're trying to make you fa-at!'

With all eyes upon me I have to go to the canteen every day and struggle with a salad. With Mum and Dad bullying me at home it is impossible not to eat, so once again the merry-go-round slows and I stop starving myself and put on a little weight.

A few months later Mum and I are watching telly together. A programme about a girl called Catherine Dunbar starts. I am riveted because the actress playing Catherine has the most beautiful long hair, and I want to grow my hair as long as that. It's a true story about a stupid girl who worries about her weight one minute and stuffs her face the next. 'What's she doing, Mum?' I ask when Catherine starts shovelling handfuls of pills into her mouth. 'She's taking laxatives,' says Mum, and I can tell from her voice that it's an awful thing to do.

'You're not going out of this house looking like a tart!' yells Dad. 'I don't look like a tart,' I protest. 'Tell him, Mum.' 'Your Dad's right, Claire,' she says. I am into Madonna, big-time, and even dress like her. I wear big crosses and chains, gloves and masses of blue eyeliner. My hair is dyed blonde and permed, and I dry it upside down for maximum effect. My cropped top shows my black bra underneath, and a tiny black skirt falls around my hip bones. 'It's barely a belt!' splutters my outraged father.

'You can't stop me,' I say, stomping back upstairs to my room where Kim and my brother's friend Kevin are waiting for me to finish getting ready. Seconds later Dad is at my bedroom door, 'Out!' he says to Kim and Kevin – you've never seen two people scarper so fast. 'If you don't take those clothes off, I'm going to rip them off you, throw petrol over them and burn them,' he says, and leaves the room. I know he means business. Crying with frustration I take off the skirt and stick on some trousers. Then I go to The Saracen's Head in Dunstable and get drunk.

Kim and I virtually live at The Saracen's Head – we're there Wednesdays, Fridays, Saturdays and Sundays. I am going through a 'what the hell' stage and get drunk on cider and snog anybody. I am still paranoid about my weight and food is a problem, but not as big a problem as getting out of the house with my Madonna outfit intact! I am having one almighty crack, and later I will look back on the year that I was 17 as being one of the happiest of my life.

I love my job. I am made a senior sales assistant and, soon after, supervisor of menswear – it has been my dream to be a supervisor and I love it. My sales team consists of Claire McCann, a full-time assistant, and a college student called Veronica who comes in on Saturdays and in the holidays. Veronica is a big girl with albino colouring and a nervous tic. She is sweet but painfully shy, and whenever anybody speaks to her she goes bright red. Claire is the complete opposite. A chatty, laughing Irish girl, she is a year older than me and has worked as a butcher in her dad's shop. She is stocky with short hair and huge owly glasses, and we get on like a house on fire.

'Once, for a laugh, my friend and I stuck our fingers down our throat to see if it worked,' says Claire one night when we are out drinking. 'What do you mean?' I ask. 'You know,' she says. 'You stick your fingers down your throat to make yourself sick.' 'Oh,' I say.

I get home, eat two Jaffa cakes, go into the bathroom, put my hair in a pony tail, turn on the cold tap, lift the loo seat and stick my index finger down my throat. Nothing happens. I try again, and graze the inside of my throat with my nail by mistake. I cough. Another jab with the finger and I cough again. My eyes start watering and the glands in my neck begin to swell. Poke, poke; cough, cough. My stomach jumps upwards towards my throat and *bleaugh* the contents hurtle through my fingers into the toilet bowl. The smell is awful, but I have to stay bent over the bowl spitting out great gobs of saliva and fumbling for the toilet paper to wipe my slippery fingers. It works alright.

Afterwards, I put down the lid of the toilet and flush. I lay my head on the grey furry loo-seat cover and listen to the deadly thoughts trickling back into my brain: 'I've got to lose some weight, I'm *so* fat.'

'I've always been a bit paranoid about my weight,' I say, joining in on a conversation that Claire is having about dieting with Janet Chin, who works in the shoe department. Claire and Janet look at me in astonishment. 'How can you be?' exclaims Claire. 'But you're so thin!' echoes Janet. 'I think I'm fat,' I say quietly, 'and I'm trying to lose a bit of weight.' In fact I am dieting like crazy and things are getting out of hand.

Other people's lives revolve around going to work, getting home from work, feeding the kids, having dinner, going out, having a crack. My world revolves around how much I weigh, how big I look, what I can eat, what I can't eat; and how much I have to eat to satisfy my parents, so they don't nag, and Mrs Sansom, so she doesn't suspend me. Food is my specialist subject and, most of all, I want rid of it.

I don't like making myself sick – I'm not very good at it, but I'm brilliant at taking laxatives. I got the idea from the 'Catherine' documentary I saw on TV last summer. Taking laxatives helped Catherine lose a lot of weight. Sure, they also helped kill her; but she was anorexic, wasn't she? I just want to lose a few pounds.

The first time I take the recommended dose: I swallow two brown Senokot pills with water and wait. They work a treat. I reckon if I increase the dose I'll get thinner, quicker.

'For God's sake,' says Claire, 'you don't need to lose any more weight. You're looking so ill. And where's your personality gone?' 'But I just feel I'm too big,' I tell her. I am quite open with my friend about my problems with food, and even tell her that I am taking laxatives. Like me, she doesn't fully appreciate the long-lasting damage that laxative abuse does to the body; she's more worried about me not eating. 'If you were as big as me you'd have to worry,' she says, 'but there's nothing of you: you don't have to diet.' She begs and pleads with me to eat, and sometimes she gets angry.

'Carry on,' says Claire crossly, as she drives me home one night in her Renault. 'Just carry on not eating. It's doing me good – I'm losing weight worrying about you!' And she is, poor girl. She's carrying all the worry and stress of seeing me not eat day after day after day. I hide it from everyone else, but let my friend glimpse what's really going on. I'm filled with guilt at what I am doing to her, and scribble her a note. *'I'm so sorry for causing you all this pain,'* I write, *'I promise I'll try to eat. I'm so scared of losing you. You're the only one who understands me, and I don't know what I'd do if you weren't my friend.'* I post it through the slats of her locker at work, the first of many insecure little notes.

Claire tells her father about me, and big gruff Matt McCann then spends hours talking to me too. He tries to coax me into eating and suggests several times that I come to live with their family. But I am trapped in a bubble of disbelief, and no one can make themselves heard above the roar in my head which says, 'You're bad, you're fat: you don't deserve to eat.'

By early 1989 I am taking 30 Senokot a day. It always has to be 30 – not 29 or 31: it's a ritual. My body has hardened to the huge doses and it now takes 12 hours for my bowels to work, so I tend to take the tablets at night. I know that if I take laxatives at 6 p.m. they'll work at 6 a.m. the following day, and my trots to the toilet will be complete before I have to go to work. I think I've got it down to a fine art.

A girl called Rosaleen, who works at British Home Stores, is getting married in Scotland. Claire and I are invited to the wedding and decide to go up the week before, stay with Rosaleen's family in Hamilton and have a bit of a holiday.

The coach to Hamilton leaves at midnight and will arrive just after six the following morning. Claire and I spend the evening getting drunk in a pub with a gang from work. At ten o'clock I swallow my laxatives in the Ladies, thinking that by the time they work I'll be safely installed at Rosaleen's. We carry on drinking until it is time to catch the coach. Then Claire and I stagger aboard, whacking other passengers on the head with our holdalls as we stumble to our seats.

A couple of hours later, horribly familiar feelings of fatigue begin to overwhelm me and my vision begins to blur. 'Oh, my God!' I think to myself, 'the laxatives are working too early!' Mixing laxatives with alcohol has been a bad move. 'Here, use my bum as a cushion,' says Claire, curling up in her seat. She has no idea I've taken laxatives – just thinks the drink has made me tired.

Sleep is impossible. I close my eyes, but rows of dots keep realigning for my inspection and sharp little stabbing pains start in my chest. My grumbling stomach begins its agonizing grind to a crescendo – 'Oh my God, here it comes!' I think. An almighty spasm shoots through me and I have just seconds to scramble over Claire and rush to the loo. The pain is excruciating – my insides seem to be cascading into the toilet along with their contents. I cling to the toilet seat and boil with a terrible fever. A high-pitched buzzing fills my ears and everything goes black. When the pain subsides and my vision clears I clean myself up as best I can, and head back to my seat, barely able to walk. 'Thank God that's over,' I say to myself. Only, with laxative abuse, it's never over and, as the coach rumbles through the night, I am forced to scuttle backwards and forwards to the disgusting toilet.

Scotland is a nightmare. It is freezing and I am forced to eat more than usual to keep out the cold and stop people commenting. I shovel down tablets at all times of day and night to make up for it. We hire a car and do a lot of sightseeing, and I am forever having to rush to the toilet. After we get back from a visit to Edinburgh Castle, I am chattering away to Rosaleen's dad when suddenly I freeze, and burst into tears. I've had a terrible accident! 'Are you okay?' says Rosaleen's father. 'Can I have a bath please?' I sob. 'It'll take a while for the water to heat up,' he says, looking bewildered. 'I'll have a cold one,' I say. 'Yes,' I hear him say, as I race up the stairs, 'Go ahead.'

Most nights we go out drinking – Claire, Rosaleen and I – and because I am so starved it only takes a couple of drinks before I'm away with the fairies. One night, after we've come in late, I go into the kitchen to get a glass of water. A tiny crumb lies on the counter, next to a sponge cake that Rosaleen was given on her hennight five days before. The cake is stale now, and nobody has thought to throw it out. 'I want this,' I think, eyeing the weeny crumb with its titchy bit of icing. Guiltily, I pick it up and stick it on the tip of my tongue. 'I need this,' I say to myself, quickly picking a little corner off the cake and popping it into my mouth. I grab a bigger piece and shove it in; then another, and another. My iron rule over my starving body snaps and I turn into an eating machine. My mind hums with nothingness, as I sit on the floor with the cake and shovel it into my emptiness.

'What the fuck are you doing?' says Claire, gazing in horror at the sight of me on the floor, ramming down the stale cake. She forces my mouth open and flicks out the cake, whacking the rest from my hands. 'Get up!' she orders. 'I want it,' I whimper helplessly, as she scoops up the cake and heads out of the back door with it to the dustbin. I stay on the floor and sob as if my heart will break. 'It's okay,' says Claire, coming back in and rushing to hold me. 'It's okay.' 'Please don't leave me,' I sniff into her shoulder. 'I won't leave you,' she says gently, rocking me in her arms, 'But you're going to die if you don't sort this out. Promise me you'll eat properly tomorrow.' 'I promise,' I say through my tears.

Next day I have toast for breakfast – oh, and 30 laxatives – but I can't manage any dinner.

'I'm hungry,' I tell the others, when we get back to the house after a night out with Rosaleen's sister. Again I am horribly drunk. In front of everyone I walk through to the kitchen and fling open all the cupboards in search of crisps, bread, biscuits, anything. I find a packet of digestives and start stuffing them down one after the other. 'Don't!' shouts Claire, but I am in a feeding frenzy and no one is getting in my way. 'Stop it!' she says, making a grab for the packet. My mouth bulging like a baby's, I spin her a look of pure hate. 'Leave me alone!' I shriek, spluttering crumbs. 'What the hell's happening to you?' says Rosaleen as she walks in, visibly shocked. 'I want those biscuits!' I yell as Claire snatches the packet. 'You're really ill,' Rosaleen whispers incredulously. 'I'm not ill!' I scream. 'Don't you want me to eat? Am I too fat?' 'We've got to go to bed now,' says Claire, trying to calm me down, but I'm not going anywhere without those biscuits. 'I'll bring them up in a minute,' says Rosaleen, snapping into action, 'Go upstairs.' So I go and Claire helps me into my nightshirt and puts me to bed. Rosaleen brings the biscuits up, sits on the bed and lets me have three. I want more, but she won't let me have any more and I bawl my eyes out.

Later, when Claire has gone to sleep, I lock myself in the bathroom and shove my fingers down my throat.

———————

'Did you eat while you were in Scotland?' asks Mum, as she drives us home from the coach station. 'Yeah,' I say. 'Did she, Claire?' she quizzes my friend, who is sitting in the back of the car. In return for her silence I've promised Claire that I will eat when I get back home. 'Yeah,' she says in a flat voice, and changes the subject.

Chapter six

'Don't bloody start that lark again,' says Mum. 'You're going to sit down and you're going to eat that.' 'I don't want it! I can't,' I protest. 'How do you think we feel? Lisa's so ill, and here you are *making* yourself ill,' says Dad. Desperate to get me to eat, my parents try various tactics. Making me feel guilty is one; issuing ultimatums is another. 'You're not going out, my girl, until you eat something,' Mum says one evening. I go to the cupboard, get out a slice of Nimble, and ram it in my mouth. 'There, I've eaten,' I say and flounce out. 'My God,' gasps Mum, 'you ate that like an animal!'

Every meal is a battle-ground, and I have honed my defence strategy. If it's shepherd's pie I eat some; then skim off the layer of mashed potato, hide my greens underneath and flatten down the mash so nobody realizes what lies below. Other bits of dinner go under my knife and fork. My most powerful allies are Drummer and our new Alsation Sheba, who lie beneath the table – their mouths ever-open – waiting to devour the enemy.

'You're going to kill yourself,' Mum and Dad keep saying. But I am trying to live: being light and empty is my way of living with myself, of surviving. Granddad hasn't touched me since the day I stopped him, but I still hate my body. I can't help thinking that if I could just rid myself of my dirty, disgusting carcass and float round the world, perhaps I'd be truly happy.

Each day I monitor my disappearance. Mum has banished the scales, so I go to work early and jump on those in the medical room before anyone else arrives. At every opportunity I sneak back in to weigh myself, and each night in the bathroom I run my body through a series of checks. We don't have a full-length mirror at home, just a half mirror above the toilet. If I stand in the bath and twist round I can watch my fingers count down my ribs in the reflection. Then I get out of the bath and stand on the toilet to inspect my bottom half. I have to be able to put my hands round my waist till they almost join. 'You're still too big though,' says the little voice, 'you still take up too much space.'

'Can I talk to you, Michael?' I say to my brother one night, after a bad day at work. I am cold and in almost constant pain from the laxatives, which frightens me. 'Mum and Dad are having a go at me about my eating again,' I say. 'Well, you're stupid,' he says matter-of-factly. 'But I'm scared of eating because I'm scared of getting big,' I say, starting to cry. 'And I'm taking laxatives,' I snivel. It is the first time I've admitted this to a member of my family and I don't really know why I choose Michael – he doesn't have a clue what laxatives are. 'They, er, make you go to the loo,' I explain hesitantly. 'Why are you taking them?' he asks incredulously. 'I feel lighter after taking them,' I mumble, 'but I'm scared because I'm in so much pain.' He looks horrified. 'I'll tell Dad,' he says, getting up to do so. 'No, don't tell Dad,' I say. 'I'll tell Mum then,' he insists. 'Don't tell either of them,' I beg. But he does.

Mum and Dad go through the roof. I just want my family to understand me, but they are frightened by what's happening to me, and fear makes them lash out. 'What are you trying to do – kill yourself and kill us with you?' yells Mum at the top of her voice. And Dad hits me across the face, hard. I go into hysterics, screaming so much that I can hardly breathe. I grab my handbag and run from the house. My brother tears down the street after me, but I am running so fast I give him the slip. Mum and Dad jump into the car and start to scour the streets.

I get as far as The Favourite pub and ring the Mc-Canns. 'It's Claire. Please help me, please!' I yell into the telephone. 'Just tell me where you are, and we'll come and get you,' says Matt who's picked up the phone. Ten minutes later I see Claire and her dad draw up outside the pub. As I come out of the building, Mum and Dad pull up as well. I run to my friend who bundles me into the back of her dad's car. 'You're coming home with us,' says Matt, getting out of the car to speak to my parents.

'Come on, Claire,' says Mum peering at me through the car window. 'You're showing us up. Come home with us now.' I bury my face in my friend's shoulder. 'What shall I do?' 'Stay. Stay with us,' she whispers. But I'm scared to: I know my parents won't like it. Matt's saying to them, 'There is no point taking her home and having a go at her. Your daughter is not well.' 'We just don't know what to do,' says Mum, starting to cry. I say goodbye to Claire and get out of the car. 'Your daughter needs help; you've got to see she needs help,' I hear Matt saying as I climb slowly into Mum and Dad's car.

Too shocked to speak, we drive home in silence, and troop into the front room. Dad sits on the organ stool, looking beaten. Mum flops on the settee, her eyes fixing on her treasured photograph collection of pet Alsations past and present. I curl up in an armchair in the corner and look at my lap. 'I am so sorry,' I say eventually, starting to cry. 'I don't want to hurt you.' 'We've got to get you sorted out,' says Mum softly. 'I'll make an appointment for you to see the doctor.'

———

'What can I do for you, Claire?' says Dr O'Donnell, looking at me over his half-spectacles. 'I'm having bad period pains,' I lie. 'Can I have some Ponstan Forte?' Period pain? I'm not even having periods! 'Of course,' he says, writing out the prescription and handing it to me. 'Thank you,' I say, picking up my handbag. 'Is there anything else, Claire?' he asks. 'No,' I reply, starting for the door.

'Can you step on the scales for me, please?' he says, casual as you like. I freeze. 'Why?' I ask. 'I just want to have a quick check on your weight,' he replies. 'No,' I say, panicking. 'Why not?' he says. 'I can't,' I reply, fear creeping into my voice. 'You look very thin to me, Claire,' he says. It suddenly dawns on me that Mum must have been to see him. 'Well, looks are deceiving!' I retort angrily. 'I'm about 8$\frac{1}{2}$

stone – that's how much I am!' 'Well, let's just check, shall we?' he says, patiently. The floodgates open – 'I can't, I can't!' I weep. He walks round the desk, guides me back to the chair and pushes a box of tissues towards me. Then, after I've dried my tears, he says softly, 'I need you to get on the scales.' So I do, and I weigh just under 7 stone.

'For your height you should be anything from a minimum of 8 stone 11 to a maximum of 10 stone 12,' he says, consulting the Body Mass Index. He points to a red bit on a chart. 'Your weight is right down here in the danger zone.' Then he takes my pulse. 'You are emaciated and your pulse is too low,' he says, making notes in my file.

'Have you heard of anorexia nervosa, Claire?' he asks, putting his pen down and eyeing me over his glasses. 'Yeah,' I reply sullenly. 'That's what you've got,' he says. But I don't believe him. 'No I haven't,' I insist. 'What makes you say that Claire?' he asks. 'Those people are really thin,' I say.

'Right,' says Dr O'Donnell finally, 'I'd like to see you every week and I am also going to refer you to the hospital, to someone who is experienced in these matters.' Hospital! 'Will I have to go to hospital?' I ask, mortified. 'You might have to,' he says gently.

'You shouldn't have told them,' says the bullying voice in my head. 'That was weak, and now they're going to make you extremely fat.' An army of people are joining forces against me and I have to do something.

I tell Mum that I'm not going to take laxatives any more; but I lie and bury them under my bedroom carpet. I start to eat more regularly. For breakfast, I have a slice of Nimble toasted with the lowest of low-fat spreads. Dinner is a bowl of Weight Watchers mine-strone soup. In the evening I have a roll with a wafer of cheese melted in the middle. It is a starvation diet; but I get away with it, because Mum and Dad know nothing about calories. They are just relieved to see me eat.

I am scared. I want to stop taking the laxatives which make me feel so ill, and I don't want to end up in hospital. In a rash moment I give all my laxatives to Claire McCann. She puts them in her locker, and the instant she shuts the door I regret it.

I spin a story to Shirley, a girl at work, and she promises to get me some laxatives when she goes out at lunch-time. On her way back Shirley bumps into Claire and hands her the tablets to give to me. Claire goes ballistic. 'Keep 'em, keep 'em!' she shouts, taking all the laxatives from her locker and throwing them at me. 'I'm sorry, I'm sorry!' I plead, scrabbling around the floor to gather up the packets and thinking, 'I've pushed her too far.' 'I can't deal with this any more!' she yells at me. 'Please don't stop being my friend,' I cry. 'I won't,' she says, calming down, 'but I can't cope any more.' 'Listen,' I say, 'I'll have a sandwich' – any-thing to pacify her. So we go up to the canteen and I eat a sandwich. Afterwards I go to the toilet. I am so intent on getting rid of the food that I don't notice that my friend has followed and can hear me throwing up.

In desperation, Claire McCann rings her GP. She gets talking to the doctor's receptionist, who says that her daughter Lesley is anorexic and has been for years. She wonders if Claire and I would like to come to her house the following night to meet Lesley.

'So you hide yourself in baggy clothes,' says Lesley, eyeing me up and down. 'I always dress like this,' I protest weakly, feeling awkward. Lesley is quite a bit older than me, and has short brown hair and massive eyes. Her top half is very thin but her legs are quite muscular because she exercises so much. 'You won't have any friends – I don't,' she says. 'They stick you in hospital where you won't be allowed visitors; you'll be made to stay in bed and they won't let you wash your hair. But,' she adds, 'your hair will fall out anyway.' It sounds barbaric. 'You'll lose everything,' she continues, 'so, stop! Stop it now while you still can.' But I don't know how.

I start going to Lesley's house on Sunday afternoons: Mum would stop me if she knew Lesley was anorexic, but she just thinks Lesley's a friend of Claire McCann's. When Lesley picks me up in her Mini, she's usually wearing a duffle coat to keep out the cold and her little nose is always red. Lesley is a hardened anorexic, but she does allow herself proper meals after she's been to aerobics: I am subsisting on fewer than 250 calories a day.

'Get in the car, skinny,' says Lesley, eyeing my stick-like legs beneath my black skirt. I am feeling cold and ill. My eyes have started to sink in their sockets and Mum and Dad are in despair. Up in Lesley's room I huddle against the radiator. She's been given a box of Quality Street. 'I like the fudge diamonds,' I say. 'Would you like one?' she says, rooting for the distinctive pink wrapper. 'I can't,' I say, as she fishes out the sweet and holds it out to me. I want it, but can't bring myself to take it. I am fat, dirty and disgusting and don't deserve anything nice. 'Go on,' says Lesley. 'I can't,' I insist. Lesley keeps on at me so, to shut her up, I say that I'll eat the sweet next Sunday. Lesley carefully sets the fudge diamond aside; and I spend the entire week fretting about it.

'God, you look awful!' exclaims Lesley, the following Sunday. We go straight up to her room and I take up my post against the radiator. Lesley hands me the fudge diamond and picks a sweet out for herself. 'Okay,' she says, 'I'm going to have this one – you have the fudge diamond.' The radiator burns into my back, but I am so cold I don't feel it. 'I can't,' I cry, tears streaming down my face. 'Okay,' she says, taking the sweet from my hand and opening it up, 'I'll get a knife and cut it in half.' She gives me half, but I am too frightened to put it in my mouth – once I start eating I mightn't be able to stop. Lesley cuts the half in quarters, but I sob and shake my head. Eventually, Lesley coaxes me into eating a bit smaller than the top of my fingernail. I feel so bad that when I get home, I have to take more laxatives.

Chapter seven

'She's too thin. She's ever so thin,' they're saying, their faces swimming above me like huge moons. I'm lying on a bed of glass and broken light-fittings while staff and a few 'let me through, I'm a nurse' customers muse over my condition. I'd been heading for the stairs up to the stock room, but they kept careering off into the distance. Patches of blackness kept invading my vision, and I couldn't breathe. 'I can't get there, I can't make it,' I thought, trying to catch sight of another member of staff. 'Dawn!' I cried, seeing the supervisor of lighting through the fog. But as she turned, my legs buckled and sent me crashing into a set of glass display shelves laden with lights. It seems I've been unconscious for 10 minutes. I am helped to the medical room, and Mrs Sansom tells me to take the rest of the week off.

'You're too ill to work,' says Dr O'Donnell when I next see him. 'Your appointment with the hospital should come through soon, but I'm signing you off work till then.' In his letter to Mrs Sansom he tactfully writes that I have digestive problems. I'm relieved not to be going back to work: even lifting a pair of slippers back onto a shelf has become an effort.

———————

'It's thicker,' I cry, my voice rising. 'What have you done to this soup? It's thicker!' 'I haven't done anything to it Claire,' says Mum. 'I can't eat it! I can't!' I yell, 'you're trying to poison me.' 'For Christ's sake, girl, look at you, look at you!' screams Mum, losing her patience. 'You're nothing but a bag of bones! And you are not leaving that table until you've eaten that soup.' So I suck each spoonful before I swallow, and spit anything slightly lumpy back into the bowl.

After that I decide I'm not going to have soup for dinner any more. Instead, I cut myself a thin slice of cheese and have a hot chocolate made with skimmed milk. I eat the cheese in a particular way. I feed half to Sheba, then nibble all the way round the rest of the cheese, and stick the little pieces to the roof of my mouth with my tongue, the better to savour the flavour. I take sips of the hot chocolate and try not to swallow the cheese until the drink is finished. It is a disgusting little ritual, but somehow it makes eating more bearable.

Off work, I establish a rigid daily routine for myself. After Mum, Dad and Michael leave for work and Lisa has gone to school, I start my stomach exercises. I lie flat on the floor, put my arms over my head and slowly raise my legs up to the count of 10, then lower them to 10. Up and down, on and on, until I ache. I shower and inspect my body and then hide it in my baggy white jogging suit. I brush my hair and great clumps fall out; I notice long strands criss-crossing my pillow.

Breakfast is at eight o'clock sharp – not a minute earlier, not a minute later. Then I clean the house from top to bottom – vacuuming every inch, dusting and polishing everything – even though the place is immaculate from the going-over I gave it yesterday. On the hour, every hour, I stop what I am doing and race around the house. I drag myself up and down the stairs five times, run into every room and round every bed, and then tear out of the back door and do 10 circuits of the garden. I finish off with 20 star-jumps. All the time I'm calculating calories in my head – '21, 22, 25' – estimating how much breakfast I've burned off. 'You've got to burn calories, you lazy cow,' hums the voice in my head. Again and again I rush to the bathroom mirror to remind myself of how ugly and revolting I am, and how much I need to lose this weight.

Lunch is on the dot of 12. Afterwards I allow myself to sit down and watch *Home and Away*. Sometimes I'll pull Sheba to me, bury my face in her coarse coat and cry. Then I'll drag myself off the settee and find an excuse to walk to the shops – I don't take the dogs, I'm too weak to hold on to them. Past the local shops I go and on to those a couple of miles away. It's such an effort. My legs either go to jelly or feel like lead weights. 'I'm tired because I'm lazy,' I tell myself. 'My legs are heavy because they're too fat.' My reflection in the shop windows proves it. I push myself through the park, muttering my mantra: 'What you eat today, you wear tomorrow.'

I spend my afternoons making the evening meal for the rest of the family – shepherd's pie or pasta, and always a dessert like apple crumble. Cooking is a test to prove that I am strong and in control of my disgusting body. When I slop food on the counter, I resist the temptation to scrape it up with my finger and lick. If I am sprinkling grated cheese on a dish and some spills over, I scoop the cheese into my hand and re-sprinkle. Sometimes I have this over-powering urge to get a big spoon and dive into the saucepan, but I keep myself in check. 'After all,' sings the voice in my head, 'a moment on the lips is a month on the hips!'

With the tea done, I run about the house some more until Dad comes home from work – it's nutty I know, but sitting down is lazy and I'm a fat bitch who needs the exercise. Mum is working as a clinic clerk at Luton and Dunstable Hospital, and at the end of the day Dad and I collect her in the car. I am al-ways relieved to haul my exhausted body into the back seat. I love the feeling of being in the car – it's warm and I have no choice but to sit still. The jour-ney signals the end of the day's activity for me be-cause, with the family home, there's no way I can race about like a maniac.

Mum takes one look at me sitting in the back of the car and gets a real strop on – nothing has changed, I'm getting worse. All the way home I worry. Is Mum going to ask me what I had to eat today? Are the others going to go on at me to have some of the meal I've made? I watch my family tuck in and feel envious, desperately wanting to do the same. But wrapped in my rituals and obsessions, I can't allow myself to have anything but my usual bread roll and Diet Coke. If I keep to the rules, I rest easier at night, knowing that I've done what I can to make myself thin. If I have something in addition to my starvation diet, I have to punish myself by taking laxatives.

My family are lucky to get a word out of me. Most of the time I hole up in my room with my tapes for company – over and over again I play the same plaintive ballads by The Carpenters, such as 'Eve'. Listening to Karen Carpenter's melancholy lyrics, I cry and cry and cry. It feels like she's the only one who understands my pain.

'I don't belong here,' I think, looking at Mum, Dad, Michael and Lisa sitting around in the front room, watching *Coronation Street* and chatting. But I don't know where I do belong. I'm withdrawing from my friends, even Claire McCann. She comes over to see me and I pretend to be happy. I crack the odd joke and laugh and maybe sing a bit. But all the while I'm thinking, 'She doesn't know me. She thinks I'm a nice person, but I'm not – I'm an evil fraud.'

'You've got to get out of the house into the real world,' says Claire McCann. 'I don't feel like going out,' I protest. 'You're coming and that's it,' she says, not taking no for an answer. So I put on a pair of jeans. They're a size 8. I thread a belt through the waistband, hoist the jeans to my waist and do the belt up on the last notch. The jeans hang off me and there is a big wodge of material at the back where my bum should be. I need Dad to make another hole in my belt really, but daren't ask because I know he'll freak. I take the belt off to see if I can do it myself, and my jeans fall to my hip bones. The sense of superiority that I feel for a split second is unreal.

In The Brewery Tap pub people are staring: they catch my eye and quickly look away. 'They think I'm too fat,' I tell myself, especially if it's a slim person looking. It doesn't occur to me that I look like something out of Belsen. I've plastered on the eye make-up and applied blusher to my cheekbones to try to make myself look half-way decent. I imagine I'm making myself look less ugly. In reality I've accentuated my skeletal features and made myself look worse, but I don't see it that way.

Claire and her sister Helen talk about the blokes in the pub and who they fancy. I am more interested in looking at the other girls. 'She's got a nice figure,' I think to myself. 'She hasn't. God, she's thin.' 'Isn't she slim?' I say to Claire. 'I'd love to be as slim as her.' Claire looks at me and says, 'To be that slim you'd have to put on at least a stone and a half.' 'Huh, she hasn't seen me with nothing on,' I think to myself. 'It's just a trick of the light that I look thinner than I really am: I know I'm really big.'

The others are drinking lager but I stick to tap water. I don't have Diet Coke just in case the barman gives me normal Coke by mistake. I won't even touch bottled water – there might be a fruit flavouring in it which equals 0.2 of a calorie! I try to get involved in the conversation but I just want to go home and listen to my music. The pub is packed and people look hot, but I am as cold as ice and feeling shaky. 'My God,' says Claire, 'you've gone blue! Sit down a minute.' My friend rushes to the bar and comes back with a blackcurrant cordial and lemonade. 'Get that down you,' she orders. Because I am scared I'm going to pass out and ruin her evening, I drink it. I make myself suffer for it though – I take laxatives for the next three days.

Most evenings I watch a bit of telly, before having yet another shower or a bath. It drives dad nuts. 'It's such a waste of hot water,' he says. But I need to wash; I really smell. For the zillionth time that day I'll check my body in the mirror. Then I'll go to my room to write my diary. It's not a proper diary, just a series of jottings in a shorthand notebook. Each entry revolves around what I've eaten that day. I tot up my calorie intake, and always add extra to be on the safe side. Next to the total I scrawl the words 'Pig', 'Fat Cow' or 'Greedy Bitch'. Then I lie freezing on my electric blanket. Three duvets, sheets and blankets can't keep the chill from my bones. I am exhausted, but sleep eludes me. I don't know that a person needs to consume around 1,100 calories a day just to be able to sleep. Reading doesn't help – with my concentration shot to pieces, thoughts of food obscure the pages. My stomach grumbles and my mind races. I go over what I've eaten, what I haven't eaten, what I'll have to eat tomorrow. Don't get me wrong, I love food – but to me it's out-of-bounds.

As I wait for sleep, I pray, 'Please God, make me slimmer tomorrow.' And I often cry. So as not to wake Lisa, I muffle my sobs with Gizmo, an old teddy bear. His fur is matted now, stuck together with years of tears. When at last I drop off, my sleep is filled with dreams of the pic 'n' mix sweet counter at Woolworths. The dreams are so vivid, I wake tasting sweets in my mouth and shaking with panic at what I've done. I grab my stomach; then realize with relief that I'm safe in bed.

———————

Mum is insistent. 'We're going to have lunch in town today, and you're going to have a cheese roll.' 'I can't, Mum,' I say, 'that's too much. If I have that I am going to be massive.' 'You're having it and that's that,' she says, firmly. 'I'm not having breakfast then,' I reply, 'and I don't have to have a roll for tea.' 'Whatever,' she sighs.

So we go to a café in town, and sit down. 'You're having a hot chocolate,' she says. 'No way!' I protest loudly. It'll be made with full-fat milk. Mum backs down – she thinks I might throw a wobbly in the middle of the café – but she orders me a cheese roll, and a sandwich for herself.

It's huge, this roll. With a thick, hard crust and so much grated cheese that it's falling out of the sides all over the plate, it's frightening to look at. I bite into it and it tastes awful. It really is disgusting, and I'm glad. Mum says her sandwich isn't very nice either. 'See,' says the little voice. 'You don't deserve it and you're not meant to have it.' So I eat the lot, just to punish myself.

Afterwards we walk round town. Dizziness fills my head and my legs seem to belong to someone else. I keep touching them to see if they are still there. 'Can we sit down, Mum?' I say, the pains in my chest making me breathless. She sits me on a wooden seat outside the town hall and I watch the pigeons squabble over bits of bread, while Mum darts into a newsagent's. She comes out with a Crunchie and insists I have a piece. I take a tiny bite, and whoosh! – it's like somebody has injected me with heroin. My energy levels soar and I race at the pigeons. They rise in clouds about my head and I giggle hysterically like an old drunk. Mum looks frightened and doesn't offer me another piece.

Chapter eight

'Are you going to weigh me?' I say suspiciously, hovering by the door. 'No, Claire,' says Dr Pinto, the consultant psychiatrist, in smooth Anglo-Indian tones. 'I am not interested in your weight; I am interested in you.' My hospital appointment has come through and Mum's come with me to the Luton and Dunstable Hospital.

Dr Pinto gestures to two chairs across the desk from his, and Mum and I sit down. 'Now what seems to be the problem, Claire?' he asks. 'Dr O'Donnell doesn't think I'm eating,' I mumble. 'What are you eating, Claire?' he asks, fixing me with his hooded brown eyes. They remind me of an eagle's eyes. I hesitate. 'She's hardly eating anything,' starts Mum. 'She collapsed at work. She can hardly walk across the front room without getting out of breath.' 'Shut up, will you!' I'm saying in my head. I feel embarrassed, like a naughty found-out little schoolgirl. Dr Pinto listens intently, punctuating each of my misdemeanours with a little nod. There's no stopping Mum. 'She's weighing herself umpteen times a day,' she says. 'We found out she's been taking laxatives.'

'Claire,' Dr Pinto interjects, 'are you aware that laxatives make you lose vital body fluids and they can unbalance your electrolytes and your potassium levels? They are very dangerous and can make you go into cardiac failure. Do you understand?' The colour drains from Mum's face and her mouth opens in a silent 'O'. 'Yeah, yeah, yeah,' I say to myself. 'It's not going to happen to me.'

'I think you need to come into the Faringdon Wing, Claire,' says Dr Pinto at the end of our appointment. No way. It's a psychiatric wing – somewhere we used to take the piss out of at school. I'll be classed as a nutter; I'll lose all my friends. 'I'll eat better at home, I promise,' I say quickly, and I mean it, I really do. 'Okay,' he says, 'I'll give you till Thursday to put on some weight, and if you don't you must come into hospital. In the meantime, I need to check your heart with an electro-cardiogram, and do some blood tests.'

Clutching my notes, I walk with Mum to the General side of the hospital where the ECG and blood tests are to be done. It's only a short distance; but I am so exhausted by the exertion, I barely register that the words 'anorexia nervosa' have been scrawled across the file. I strip down to my knickers and lie on a bed. The nurse smothers my chest with cold jelly-like stuff and applies little black suction pads which are connected with wires to a machine which reads my heart rhythms. 'Do you think I'm fat?' I ask the nurse. She looks down at me. 'My dear,' she says, 'you are tiny. A good meal is what you need.'

In another room, a different nurse tries to extract blood from me. Unable to find a vein, she jab

jab jabs the needle into my arm. I am so cold and undernourished, my veins have sunk towards my bones and all but disappeared. 'Have a sweet, dear,' says the nurse. 'It might make you feel better.' If she had troubled to look at my notes, she'd have realized that's the last thing a sweet would do. Eventually she manages to find some blood to siphon off into her test tube, and Mum and I go home.

At home I dutifully eat a sandwich, just as I promised, but by tea-time I'm back in the old routine. I crawl into my all-in-one blue fleecy tracksuit – I call it my babygrow – and go to bed early. I am lying there, trying to shut out the thought that I'm going to end up in the loony bin, when Dad pokes his head round the door.

'Hello, sweetheart,' he says. He's bought a magazine filled with low-calorie recipes. 'What if we get Mum to make you one of these?' he says, sitting on the bed and turning the glossy mouth-watering pages. I shake my head. 'I can't,' I say. 'Claire, please; sweetheart, please,' he says, his voice beginning to crack. 'It's breaking my heart seeing you like this.' 'Dad, I can't,' I say, starting to cry. 'I love you and I wish I could, but I can't.' Tears forge their way down my father's face and splash onto the shiny pages. And if I could have eaten for anyone, it would have been for my Dad that day.

Four days later Mum and I are back in Reception waiting to see Dr Pinto. Mum's flicking through a *Woman's Own* magazine. She points to a picture of a steamed pudding. 'Would you like me to make you that?' she asks gently. 'No,' I say coldly, and turn away. I can't sleep at all now and I'm feeling like death.

In Dr Pinto's office I try my best to look alert, but the doctor's features keep rearranging themselves in front of my eyes, and I'm finding it hard to follow what he's saying. 'How are you?' asks Dr Pinto. 'Fine, thank you,' I say automatically. 'Claire,' he says, 'I have had the results of your ECG, and it would be irresponsible of me not to tell you that you're dying.' I snap to attention; Mum's face crumples and falls. 'Your body has eaten all of its muscle and it is now attacking your heart,' Dr Pinto continues. 'If we do not get food into you immediately, you may go into heart failure. Do you understand what I am saying, Claire?' I nod dumbly and think, 'He's going a bit over the top, isn't he?' 'I would like you to come into hospital,' Dr Pinto continues. 'No,' I protest weakly. 'I think you need to come into hospital, Claire,' he says, adding mysteriously, 'you do understand that if you do not come in, we have ways of getting you into hospital without your say-so?'

I have no choice. Dr Pinto wants me to go into hospital, so does Dr O'Donnell. If I don't give in, it seems I'll be sectioned under the Mental Health Act and made to go in. Mum and Dad are begging me to admit myself – their pleas reaching a crescendo and erupting in floods of tears. I am scared of hospital but, at the same time, longing for someone else to take charge. I am like a circus-trainer in the lion's den. For years I've been cracking the whip over my unruly charge. But the lion has grown big and hungry, and I'm frightened that if I don't get some back-up, I'll lose control and he'll bite off my head. 'Okay,'

I say, 'I'll go in.' Mum cries some more with relief then, wiping her eyes, she rings the hospital.

Later that evening Mum drives me round to Claire McCann's. I sit on Claire's bed, my back propped against the wall. I don't seem to be able to breathe and talk at the same time, and my eyes keep closing. 'I'm going into hospital,' I say. My friend bursts into tears and hugs me. 'Thank God!' she cries. I cry too. 'I'm scared,' I sob. 'I know,' says Claire, 'but it's for the best. You can't deal with this. This thing's too big for you and me to handle.'

Over the weekend I get my stuff together: I pack Gizmo and lay an emergency supply of laxatives under the cardboard bottom of my bag – 'just in case'. I read the glossy brochure about the Faringdon Wing. It looks okay really – a bit like a hotel. The nurses wear ordinary clothes instead of uniforms; and the patients wear day clothes – they are not confined to nighties and pyjamas – or straightjackets for that matter! There is a table-tennis table and dartboard in the main lounge. It says discos are held regularly, and there are activities like art, woodwork and pottery. The bedrooms look nice, and in one of the photographs people are having their hair and nails done. There are gardens to walk in, and even a tennis court.

––––––––––

The leaflet is a load of crap. Predominantly brown and orange, the place stinks of piss. The other patients shuffling around all seem two sandwiches short of a picnic and have those giveaway pudding-basin haircuts. I've never seen psychiatric patients in the flesh before, and I'm really frightened. A little

Filipino nurse called Editha takes Mum and me up two flights of stairs, straight through the double-doors of Ward 17 and into one of two rooms marked 'Interview Room'. There a man roots through my bag and confiscates my razors. 'Do you think I'm a fucking psychopath?' I shout angrily. 'Claire!' Mum frowns.

Then Editha shows us around. She indicates the nurses' station. It's opposite the entrance where we came in, so no one can get on or off the ward without passing its window. The ward is a quadrangle with rooms off it to the right and left. A corridor runs round like a right-angled racing track.

The ward consists of eight single rooms and two male and two female dormitories, each containing four beds, four lockers and four built-in cupboards. There's a smoking room, a day-room with a TV burbling in one corner and a small activity room – presumably where the art, woodwork and pottery take place. Near the nurses' station is a small locked kitchen, a seating area and a dining table.

I am to sleep in one of the tired-looking single rooms. I sit on the bed and look round at the tatty built-in cupboard, the institutional bedside locker, the washbasin and the narrow single bed with its thin green cover. The window is hung with faded floral print curtains and looks out on to the car park. My eyes prick with unhappiness. This is the re-ality of Ward 17 – admission ward for acute psychi-atric patients.

'I can't stay here, Mum,' I say, starting to cry. 'I'll go to hospital, but to the General side. I can't stay here.' Mum asks if I can be moved, but I'm not allowed – mine isn't a physical problem, but a psychiatric one which causes physical complications. I am inconsolable. Mum sits on the bed, puts her arm round me and cries with me.

Later, after Mum has gone, Editha tells me that I have a case conference with Dr Pinto, and directs me to a room near Ward 17. 'Come in,' says Dr Pinto as I tap on the door. I am expecting to see just Dr Pinto, but I open the door and at least half a dozen pairs of eyes swivel in my direction. In the middle of the seated circle sits Dr Pinto. 'Hello, Claire. Come and sit down,' he says, gesturing to an empty chair next to him. This, apparently, is a case conference. 'How do you feel?' 'Do you feel in control when you don't eat?' 'Do you this?' 'Do you that?' There are no introductions, no niceties – these doctors, psychiatrists, nurses, social workers, or whatever they are, launch in with questions from every angle. As I struggle to find an answer to one question, a different mouth chimes in with another query. They are relentless and I'm reduced to tears. I feel like a slimy little specimen under a microscope.

I pray hard that night. 'Dear Lord Jesus Christ, please let this whole thing be just a nightmare. Please let me wake up at home.' Trouble is, it's very very real.

'Morning, Claire,' says Editha in her sing-song voice, the following morning. She's brandishing a set of scales. 'I have to weigh you today.' She sets down the scales. I have no choice but to step on to them. 'God, I'm so fat,' I think to myself. 'I need to lose weight. I need to be $6\frac{1}{2}$ stone.'

Dr Pinto comes to see me in my room. He is armed with a piece of graph paper on which are drawn two axes – one showing weights, the other dates. He draws three lines across the page which graduate up to 8½ stone. 'Okay,' he says, 'this is what's going to happen. Your goal is to get to 8½ stone.' 'Like hell,' I think to myself, beginning to hate Dr Pinto with a vengeance. 'You will be required to gain one pound a week,' he continues, as if it is the easiest thing in the world. 'If you gain weight you will be allowed to go home for visits. If your weight drops below the top line – which it will if you fail to put on a pound a week – you will lose the freedom to go out of hospital; and if the weight drops below the second line you will lose your room and have to sleep in a dormitory. If it drops below the third line you won't be allowed visitors.' This is my 'behavioural programme' and it works on a privilege/punishment basis; and it seems things I took for granted – like sleeping in a room of my own, walking in the hospital gardens, going out shopping, and having visitors – are in fact privileges. My mistake!

I meet my keyworker. Her name is Anne. She's wearing trousers and a red jumper and her belt hangs loosely about her waist. I look her up and down and hate her on sight because she is skinny. Anne is in charge of my care and I am supposed to communicate with her – only, I don't. 'I'm fat,' I say. 'But you're not fat,' she replies. 'But I *feel* fat,' I insist. Round and round in circles go our conversations, getting nowhere.

Mum and Dad are going spare. 'What are you doing for her?' they berate the nursing staff. 'Claire's eating even less here than she was at home!' It's true. The nurses call me out of my room for meals. But I won't eat a thing. I pour myself a cup of tea and take it back to my room, where I stay. My room is a bit more homely now. I have my stereo and Carpenters tapes; Mum and Dad have brought in my duvet from home and the black-and-white TV, and cards from friends and family are beginning to arrive. Because I won't touch the hospital food, each night Mum brings in a flask of hot chocolate – made with skimmed milk – and my usual roll with its sliver of cheese.

I'm so angry. The nurses say I've lost 7 pounds, but there isn't any consistency in the weighing process. I am weighed at all times of the day and night, sometimes with my clothes on, sometimes in my underwear, on different sets of scales – either the OAP-type that you sit in or else the sort you stand on. Because I'm never weighed at the same time or in the same way I am suffering; I'm losing my privileges and it just isn't fair – I feel abused all over again. Dr Pinto has told me the order in which I will lose my privileges; but *he* doesn't implement the programme – the nursing staff do and they keep changing the rules. One minute I'm allowed out, the next I'm not; one minute I'm shunting my bed out of my room and into a dormitory, the next I'm told to wheel it back again. When people come to visit me they never know where to find me. It's becoming a joke – a bad one.

I can't get used to the other patients: the recovering alcoholics who shake like jellies and cry all the time; and the scruffy old guy with depression who keeps creeping up behind me and planting kisses on my face. 'You little doll,' he says before releasing me and walking away heeheeheeing manically. And there's Mark. He's 21 and recently lost his girlfriend in a car accident. We started off having a laugh, saying we were going to knot sheets together and escape out of the window to Cinderella's Nightclub. But now he's shoving letters under my door saying he loves me and that I'm the only one who can help him. It makes me nervous.

I'm always scared that someone's going to walk in on me when I'm having a bath. There is no lock on the door, and I usually try to persuade a nurse to stand guard for me. There's no shower in the ladies' bathroom, and if I want to wash my hair I have to use the shower in the men's, which is even more nerve-wracking.

I'm frightened when patients flip out – which happens on a regular basis. Screaming and shouting, they are usually propelled to the seclusion room by a clutch of nurses, jabbed in the bum with a sedative injection through their clothes, and locked in. The first few times I see this happen I am petrified; I scuttle back to my room and shut the door, convinced I'm next. I've seen the seclusion room: it has nothing in it apart from a bare mattress and a window that doesn't open.

'Where's my mum? Where's my mum?' I am screaming. From the far end of the ward I've caught sight of my parents leaving. By the time I reach the nurses' station they are gone. Propped against the door frame, I catch sight of a Sainsbury's bag containing my usual flask of hot chocolate and roll and begin to bawl. 'That's it,' I think, 'they've abandoned me;

Mum and Dad have finally had enough.' Trying to calm me down, the charge nurse takes me back to my room, and explains that I can't see my mum because I've lost weight. Nobody told me!

I am devastated. I crouch behind the door of my room with Gizmo soaking up my tears. All night I'm rocking and crying, rocking and crying. That's where Dr Pinto finds me the following morning when he is on his rounds. 'Why are you crying, Claire?' he says, squatting down next to me. 'Why the fuck do you think I'm crying?' I spit. 'My mum and dad aren't here and I hate it and want to go home.' 'If you start to gain a little weight you may feel a little better. But you are not well enough to go home, Claire,' he says, and leaves.

Perhaps he realizes how badly banishing Mum and Dad has affected me, because that evening they come down as usual, and I can see them; but they are not allowed to bring me food. I have to start eating what is on the food-trolley like everybody else, and to make matters worse I have to eat at the dining table with the loonies. 'Go on, Claire,' encourages Mum, 'you can do it.' So I go to the door of my room and peer round the corner. 'That's disgusting,' I think to myself. I haven't even seen the food. I am nauseated by the sight of the other patients *queuing* for food. They look like a troop of dirty circus animals waiting to be fed. 'I don't need to do that to survive,' I say, my grip on reality unravelling a little more.

I slip back into my room only to find Anne bearing down on me, demanding that I get something from the trolley and eat it at the table, even if it is just soup and bread. 'Go on,' says Mum, 'I'll wait for you.'

I can tell the soup isn't low calorie, and the bowl is huge. Oh, and the person serving has deliberately troweled an extra pasting of butter on the bread specially for me, I can tell. I walk to the table as slowly as I can, putting off the moment when I have to put the soup into my mouth. Only it isn't soup, is it? I know, I can tell. It's a humungous bowl full of millions and trillions of fat-laden molecules that are going to make me big. God, just think of the calories – thousands of them!

I sit down at the table, pick up the spoon and shudder at what I am about to do. 'Are you anorecthic?' shouts the schizophrenic girl with a lisp, across the table. 'No,' I say coldly. 'Well you look anorecthic,' she says. I eat the soup because I have to, then go back to my room and weep.

Chapter nine

'You've got to get better, so you can be my bridesmaid,' laughs Katrina who's come to visit me. 'I can't
get married without you!' Katrina lives a couple of
doors down, and I've known her all my life. She's
getting married in August and has asked me to be
chief bridesmaid. I suppose she's trying to cheer me
up, give me something to get well for. I visualize the
dress hanging up in 'Always The Bridesmaid', the
bridal shop owned by Mum's friend Lily. It's an off-
the-shoulder, shiny lemon confection, with a
nipped-in waist and a full skirt with lace at the bottom. I've had one fitting – the size 10 was way too
big and Lily is taking it in. 'But it's not going to fit,
is it?' I think in a panic. 'Not if the nurses and doctors make me fat!'

   'What's an 18-year-old doing in a psychiatric
unit?' says Nicky, the nurse escorting me to the
shops. It's a few days before Easter and I've been allowed out shopping under escort to buy Easter eggs
to take home at the weekend. 'You've got your
whole life ahead of you,' Nicky goes on. 'Why don't

you just eat something and get out of here? You don't want to spend the rest of your life in a place like this, do you?' 'I do want to get out,' I say, 'And on Easter Day I'm going to eat some fudge.' But when it comes to it, I'm not allowed to go home because I've lost too much weight, and I only manage one square of fudge.

'If Claire doesn't improve they're thinking of sending her to a special unit,' says one of the male nurses to Mum one day when she's visiting. 'What sort of unit?' she asks. He starts to tell us and Mum and I can't believe our ears. It's a place where patients have to earn their privileges. And a bed is classed as a privilege! Each patient is shut in a room with no windows. There is nothing in the room; the patient has to earn the right to have a bed by putting on weight. There is nowhere to be sick, and if you did vomit nobody would clear it up. You are watched 24 hours a day and can't go to the toilet unaccompanied. Mum and I look at one another in horror. It sounds barbaric – you wouldn't treat an animal like that. 'No way,' says Mum firmly. 'Claire's not going to a place like that.' I breathe a sigh of relief.

My weight is yo-yoing. I am eating more now because I have no choice, but as soon as I feel I'm too big I do something about it. I pretend to eat my meals, smuggle the food into my handbag or secrete bits up my sleeve. Then I lob it out of my bedroom window: once I obscured the windscreen of a beautiful XR3i in the car park with egg mayonnaise on brown. Or I go downstairs to Ward 18 and have a tinkle on the piano. When no one's looking, I lift the lid and softly empty the contents of my sleeves onto the little hammers inside. Across the road from the hospital is a newsagent's, a cashpoint and – joy of joys – a chemist! I'll wheedle my way out of hospital, saying I want to buy a magazine at the newsagent's, then go to the cashpoint, get out some money and pop into the chemist to stock up on laxatives. Back at the hospital I hide the tablets in my handbag, and after I've swallowed them, I take the empty packets on a walk round the garden and chuck them in the litter bin.

'Claire, will you stop; will you stop, stop stop stop!' screams the crippled schizophrenic at the bottom of the stairs. He's trying to make a phone call but all he can hear is this mad marathon runner pounding up and down the stairs between Ward 17 and Ward 18 below. I'm not allowed to exercise and am supposed to use the lift not the stairs to Ward 18, because walking uses up precious calories. 'Bollocks to that,' says the voice in my head, 'go for the burn!'. I've eaten quite a lot today and even had some chocolate, and I think I've really ballooned. I collapse in a heap at the top of the stairs just as two nurses respond to the cries of the man marooned in his wheelchair. I'm carried off to my room and told to stay in bed for an hour.

———

'How are you doing?' says Anne, poking her head round the door. I'm sitting in my room with my visitors – Claire McCann, Dad, Auntie Pat who is Mum's sister, and her husband Uncle Sid. 'Fine,' I say. 'Are you eating?' asks the nurse. 'Yes,' I answer mechanically. 'She probably sticks her bleedin' fingers down her throat and throws it up though,' says Dad, who's never very tactful at the best of times. I am horrified – he's made me look dirty and disgusting in front of Auntie Pat and Uncle Sid. Howling, I run from the room. Claire follows and finds me sobbing in the toilet. 'Your dad was out of order,' she says hugging and comforting me. 'But come on. You can do this.' Then she chuckles, and says jokingly, 'What you need is a good drink!' What a great idea! 'Please take me out,' I say. 'How can I?' asks Claire. 'We'll do it,' I insist. 'It'll do me the world of good; please.'

So one evening Claire arrives to sneak me out. We sit in my room for a while, trying to suppress our giggles and make it look like a normal visit. The nurses have no inkling that outside the Faringdon Wing Claire's sister Helen is revving up the getaway car! I'm thrilled at the excitement of it, but poor Claire is wetting herself. At the end of Claire's visits I usually walk her down to Reception where we sit and chat for a while. So we leave the radio on in my room, shut the door and walk down the two flights to Reception. At five o'clock the receptionist goes off duty, so there's no one to see me walk out of the front door and dive into Helen's car in hysterics. We whizz out of the hospital gates with the music turned up loud, cackling with laughter.

'What are you doing here?' asks Sally, the barmaid at The Halfway House in Dunstable. 'Aren't you supposed to be in hospital?' 'I've run away,' I slur conspiratorially. I've downed a couple of Lambruscos which have gone straight to my head. Sally used to work with Mum, but I know she won't tell. 'You bugger,' she says laughing. 'Get back there!'

An hour after we've done the bunk, Claire and Helen drop me back at the entrance to the Faringdon

Wing. My cheeks are bright red and I'm as drunk as a skunk, but somehow I manage to sneak back to my room without being detected.

An hour later I am in agony. 'Mum, I'm in pain,' I whimper into the payphone. I'd taken half a tube of laxatives before going out, and the Lambrusco is speeding up their effect. Hazy with tablets and booze I put the phone down on Mum, drag myself back to my room where I lie on the bed clutching my stomach. Poor Mum; she doesn't have a clue what's going on. Frantic, she rings the nurses who come to my room to see what's wrong. 'Have you taken anything, Claire?' says the night-sister. I am so confused and in so much pain I don't think of lying. 'Laxatives,' I reply, handing over the remainder in the tube. She gives me a large white tablet which takes the pain away, but I spend all night on the loo.

After that my handbag is searched for tablets every day, and if I want to go for a wander a nurse has to come with me. Then they start clamping down on my exercising, and I'm not allowed down to Ward 18 to use the piano. I piss myself laughing when the nurse tells me that – it seems playing the piano uses up too many calories! One lovely day when the other patients are being taken out for a walk, I'm told I can only go in a wheelchair. There's no way I'm being pushed in a wheelchair! I sulk and stay in my room.

Occasionally Granddad comes to visit. He sits by my bed and cries into his white handkerchief. 'I'm sorry,' he says, 'I'm so sorry.' 'Your Granddad's heartbroken that you're in hospital,' Mum and Dad keep telling me. 'He really cares about you.' I am sure he does, but he knows and I know there's another reason for his tears. To tell the truth it freaks me out to have him sitting sobbing by my bedside: it makes me feel guilty and bad for upsetting him.

One day, after Granddad's been, Claire McCann comes to give me a manicure. Heads bent close together we're deep in conversation. 'There's got to be more to this than slimming,' Claire is saying, as she often does, trying to make sense of my illness. My heart starts pumping, so fast that I think it might jump out of my throat. 'You're not a vain person.' Claire goes on shaping my long nails with the emery board. 'There's got to be more to this than wanting to be thin.' Suddenly I want to tell. Suddenly I want Claire to know why I hate my body so much.

'If I tell you something will you promise not to tell?' I say. 'Yes,' she says softly, looking up. 'Not Mum and Dad or anybody?' I say, gripping her hands. 'I promise,' she says. I can feel my mouth turning down at the corners and tears collecting in my eyes. 'Tell me,' she says gently, as drops begin to squeeze out down my cheeks. I take a deep breath, 'You know Granddad?' I say. 'Yes,' she replies. 'He abused me,' I say, my words barely audible. 'Oh, my God!' cries Claire, dropping the emery board and pulling me towards her in a hug. 'Oh,' she sobs, 'I just couldn't understand what was wrong with you. I just knew there had to be a reason behind this. I knew this was more than a slimming thing.'

We cling together, our hair wet with one another's tears. Then she pulls herself together and says with conviction, 'You've got to tell Dr Pinto.' 'I can't,' I mumble. 'You've got to,' she insists. 'I can't tell anyone. I'll break up the family,' I say. 'They don't have to know. Everything's confidential. Promise me you'll tell him,' she says, making me look her in the eye, 'promise.'

'My friend told me to tell you that I've been sexually abused by a member of the family,' I say as fast as I can, at my appointment with Dr Pinto a day or two later. 'Right, Claire,' he says, laying down his pen, 'I think we need to start again. Which family member was it?' he asks gently, his face inscrutable. 'I'm not telling you,' I say firmly, looking into my lap. 'Why aren't you telling me, Claire?' he says. 'Because I'd be betraying the family,' I say uneasily. 'Do *you* not feel betrayed Claire?' he says in his measured voice. 'I don't want to talk about this anymore,' I say, getting up and stalking out of his office.

There's a new girl on the ward. She looks about the same age as me. Her family are settling her into her room and she's crying her eyes out. As soon as they leave I'm going to introduce myself and try to cheer her up. 'Hi,' I say. 'I know it's not very nice in here, but my name is Claire.' 'Samantha,' the girl replies shortly. She's Irish, and quite big. 'What are you in here for?' I ask. 'Depression and bulimia nervosa.' 'What's that?' I ask. 'Well,' she says uneasily, 'I eat and throw up, eat and throw up.' 'Oh,' I say, 'a bit like me. But I don't really eat; they keep making me eat.' 'Oh God,' she says, and I can hear the distaste in her voice, 'you're anorexic, aren't you?' It's my turn to feel uneasy. 'Well, that's what they say,' I reply, 'but I don't think so.' 'Well, that's the fucking problem,' she says, her voice strident. 'You don't think so. That's why you're here!' After a few moments she turns away. 'You're upsetting me,' she says. 'Can you go please?' I leave the room crying – I want to be her friend, to help her. I don't understand that the one thing a bulimic cannot stand is an anorexic. In my thinness, I embody the sort of control that Samantha wishes she had over her body.

———————

March slips into April and, as the nurses become stricter, I become sneakier. In the past I've noticed that if I drink a mug of tea, it will make me – in my emaciated state – two pounds heavier. In the hours I spend twiddling my thumbs on the ward, I devise a plan. What if I consume huge quantities of liquid before I'm weighed? I've managed to convince Dr Pinto of the unfairness of weighing me at different times on different scales in various different states of undress. So I know that I am now always weighed first thing in the morning. So little by little I teach my body to hold huge amounts of liquid. I ask all my friends and relatives to bring in bottles of Diet Coke and stash them in my cupboard. I start drinking at two in the morning and every hour I drink a litre of Coke or water until half-past seven when they weigh me. The liquid swishes about inside me, and when I poke my stomach it emits strange subterranean sounds. My abdomen eventually turns rock-hard and feels like it's about to burst. I'm desperate to pee, but more desperate not to. The pain is unbelievable. I've got to go to the loo. I'll just let a little bit out – oooh, the pain's scorching! Oh, how I want to let it all go but I summon all my willpower, all my control, stop the flow and hang on, and on and on.

It's worth it. I was 7 stone 5 yesterday, but I'm 7 stone 13 today. 'Have you done something to manipulate your weight?' says Editha, eyeing me with suspicion. 'No,' I say, all innocence. But she wants to make sure, so she watches me for a good hour to see whether or not I have to rush to the loo. I want to alright; but I don't. My head hurts and I feel dizzy and disorientated. I don't realize that I've consumed more than enough fluid to drown myself.

———

I've been in hospital for almost a month. I've told Dr Pinto that my programme is unrealistic, and together we've devised a new agreement. If my weight gets to 8 stone I'll be released from hospital and can go back to work, as long as I attend his outpatients' clinic each week. If I slip below 8 stone, but remain above 7 stone 12, I have to come back into hospital but can still go to work. Below 7 stone 12, I have to stay in hospital and can't work.

I do my best to eat. I don't want to stay in hospital a minute longer than I have to. I ask Mum to bring up some of Grandma's apple pie. I eat a huge helping just before I go to sleep – the later I eat the more ballast there'll be in my tummy for tomorrow. Then as usual I do the drink trick.

'Here goes,' I say, jumping on the scales the following morning. The needle flickers and settles. Indiscernibly, I lean forward a little to push it up a fraction more. From where I stand it says 7 stone 13, but to the others standing opposite I've reached 8 stone. 'Yeah, yeah, yeah!' I yell and jump off the scales quick-smart. I'm free! Before I can rush off and start packing my things, Dr Pinto comes up to see me, to make sure I understand our agreement. He explains that I am to have a week at home before coming back in to be weighed. If my weight is satisfactory, I will be issued with a certificate to say I'm fit for work.

I'm eager to get back to work. They've changed the uniform while I've been away. I collect my brand new striped pinafore dress in a size 10 and go and have my hair permed. I feel quite healthy and am elated to be out. Despite rigging the scales, I have put on a few pounds and my eating pattern is better. Being in hospital has got me out of the habit of my starvation diet, and I've allowed myself to increase my intake a little. But I'm still rigid and obsessive about what I eat.

Breakfast is two slices of toast and Marmite and three tablespoons of Alpen with four tablespoons of skimmed milk. Mum never buys skimmed milk and if I haven't had a chance to get some, I pour a little of the full-fat stuff into a mug and water it down, then put it in the fridge to chill. For dinner I have an apple and a sandwich made without butter on brown Nimble bread with egg and Waistline salad cream or onion and cheese – grated so it looks more. For tea I'll have a couple of potatoes, vegetables and chicken baked in the oven with the skin removed.

After a week I go back to the Faringdon Wing. I see one of the doctors under Dr Pinto. I hop on the scales. They say 7 stone 12. But the doctor hasn't read the terms of my discharge properly. He's writing down my weight when I notice on his desk the certificate which says I'm fit for work. 'Is that my certificate?' I say, brightly, picking up the piece of paper. 'Thanks very much. Bye.' And I'm out of there. The doctor doesn't stand a chance. He must have noticed Dr Pinto's 8-stone rule after I've gone because he's ringing home, he's ringing work, he's ringing Mum at work at the hospital. 'She's got to come back,' he says. 'She's under 8 stone.'

'Please Mum, don't make me go back,' I beg. 'I promise I'll be good; I promise I'll eat. Honestly, sending me back will do more harm than good.' As far as she knows I've put on almost a stone, so she lets me stay.

Chapter ten

'Hi Claire, you look a lot better,' says Matt McCann, who hasn't seen me since I went into hospital. 'Oh God,' I think, 'he means I'm fat!' Claire and I have just come back from a morning's shopping and it's way past dinner-time. 'You've got to have something to eat,' says Claire. 'What do you want?' 'Egg in salad cream sandwich,' I reply, adding 'but I'll do it.' It has to be Waistline salad cream – 13 calories per table-spoon – and I have to make it. 'No,' she says firmly, '*I'll* make it.' She's trying to get a point across, trying to get me to trust somebody else to make me food. I let her get on with it, but watch her like a hawk to make sure she doesn't put too little or too much fill-ing in the sandwich. It has to be just right.

'Oh!' cries Claire, staring at me in horror, 'your lips have gone blue! Stop eating a minute and have a hot drink.' I'm used to regular meal-times in hospi-tal and usually have dinner a couple of hours earlier than this. I don't know if that's got something to do with it, but I feel okay. I don't *feel* blue. I sip the tea and Claire is relieved to see my lips return to their

MY BODY, MY ENEMY

normal colour. She brings out a packet of chocolate cup-cakes and offers me one. I want to taste it, passionately. I allow myself to. I peel the thick chocolate icing from the sponge cake and set it to one side. I eat the sponge, savouring every crumb. Then I dunk the chocolate icing in my tea. Mmm, heaven! I really enjoyed that and now I'm annoyed with myself. It's made me start wanting things I know I shouldn't have. God, where's my control?

It's summer and I'm spending a lot of time in The Clarence pub with Claire. She introduces me to Martin, one of the barmen. He's from Oldham and new in town. I like his sense of humour and his northern accent. 'Do I 'eck!' he always says. After closing-time a crowd of us usually go to The Hatters nightclub and Martin comes too. The Hatters is a dive on three floors – you only ever go there in jeans, a T-shirt and a pair of trainers because you usually get a plastic glass of lager chucked over you. I am back on the cider and the drink affects my control: I'm unable to stop myself going for a late-night curry with the rest of the crowd. I eat a lot but somehow I'm never full up. In fact, the more I eat the more I want to eat. I don't realize that I'm trying to satisfy a hunger not for food, but for love and understanding.

My weight creeps up to 10 stone. I inspect myself in the mirror at every opportunity. My hip bones, which are usually prominent, are well and truly covered and my belly is protruding – I am the shape of a pear. Claire and I are going on holiday to Gran Canaria with her sister Helen and a friend. I try to diet before I go, but I just seem to be getting bigger. I have another fitting for the dreaded bridesmaid dress, and it's not just tight – it won't even do up! Having taken it in, poor Lily's going to have to let it out again. I hide myself in long T-shirts and leggings. People keep coming up to me and saying how good I look. Apparently I'm blooming and my skin is glowing. All I see when I look in the mirror is a lazy fat cow.

We share an apartment in Gran Canaria. Claire and I hate cigarettes so we ban Helen and her friend from smoking indoors. A group of lads moves in next door and we get chatting to them by the pool. I am wearing my bikini and, being the biggest girl in the group, feel very self-conscious. I've already told the lad who's talking to me that I'm trying to lose a few pounds – because that's what he must be thinking. He lights a cigarette. 'It's bad for your health,' I tell him. 'It stops you eating though,' he says. 'Sorry?' I say, all ears. 'Didn't you know that smoking suppresses your appetite and helps you lose weight?' 'Let's try one then,' I say – I'm hooked.

Back from holiday, I start going out with Martin the barman. He is short, balding and, at 31, 12 years older than me. I notice that he can get moody when he's had a drink. I don't know why I'm going out with him really. He makes me laugh, but we don't really communicate as such – in fact, about the only thing we've got in common is that we smoke! He knows I've been ill and that I've spent time in hospital and he seems to understand. I do his head in sometimes – 'Am I fat? I'm too big, aren't I? Do you think I need to lose weight?' On and on I go. 'There's nothing wrong with you,' he says. 'You're fine.'

Martin's flat is round the corner from The Clarence: it comes with the job and he has it to himself. We kiss there but that's about it. He's tried to go further, but I've told him that I don't want to have sex because of something that happened to me when I was younger. He seems to accept the situation. He's bought a poster of a girl in a pair of knickers. She's lifting up her top and it hides her face. Her nipples are covered but you can just see the bottom part of her boobs. 'I bought that because it reminds me of you,' he says. 'Why?' I ask defensively. 'Because you're protective of your body and don't let anybody see it.' I feel embarrassed – the picture looks dirty to me.

I'm going out all the time now. I race home from work, grab something to eat and then I'm off. I am wild and rebellious and my social life means more to me than my family. I barely speak to Mum, Dad, Michael or Lisa, and they don't know what to say to me – I am so touchy, I am likely to bite their heads off. I stay out all night and don't bother to tell Mum and Dad where I am. I'm drinking a lot, the weight is piling on and I hate myself. Hatred gives me an attitude. The nice, quiet, obliging girl has become a hard cow with a vicious tongue. 'Do you mind?' I lash out, if somebody accidentally pushes against me in The Hatters. When they apologize I say, 'Yeah, well, don't do it again.' I'm fed up with working at British Home Stores which is old-fashioned and bores me to tears. I start looking for another job.

'You look brilliant,' says Lisa Duxbury, who's come over from Jersey where she's working in a hotel. The last time I saw her I was emaciated and in hospital. We go up to The Clarence and then after closing we go to The Good Good Chinese restaurant in Luton. Lisa and I are chatting over our meal. I'm having my usual – chicken fried rice, curry sauce and chips. 'That hardly touched the sides,' I say to Lisa. 'Can I have the same again, please?' I ask a passing waiter. Lisa looks at me in astonishment. 'What are you doing?' she says. 'Nothing,' I reply and change the subject. The food arrives and I devour the lot, fast. Lisa watches in horror and starts to cry. 'Claire,' she says, 'what's happening to you?' I'm angry now, pissed off with myself for pigging-out, annoyed with Lisa for going on about it. 'I'm tired,' I say bad-temperedly, 'I'm going home.' I fling some money down on the table, walk out of the restaurant, hail a cab and jump into it, leaving Lisa sitting at the table. When I get home I go straight to the bathroom and make myself sick.

Next day I'm on a real guilt trip: Lisa's one of my best friends, I hadn't seen her for a long time and I've been a complete bitch. I phone her and say I'm sorry, and she says it's okay; but I hate myself. I punch myself, punch my pillows, punch the wall. I am full of anger – I don't know where it's all coming from, or what to do with it, and I'm lashing out at myself and, worst of all, at the people I love. I don't realize that it stems from what was done to me as a child and that it should be directed at one person and one person only – the man who ruined my life.

What a nightmare! Lily's let out the dress, but it won't go near me. She's talking about inserting some more material. I'm so ashamed. I'm almost 11 stone now and loathe myself. When I catch sight of my reflection in the fitting-room mirror, I see a fairy elephant. I panic and make myself sick at every opportunity, but the weight sticks stubbornly to me. By the day of Katrina's wedding I'm convinced I'll be walking down the aisle in my knickers and bra, as I know the damn dress won't fit.

Well it does, just. The zip's under a lot of strain and my boobs are squashed by the bodice. 'You look wonderful,' says Dad, snap-snapping with his Instamatic. When the photos are developed he selects the best one, has it blown up and framed, and displays it proudly in the front room. I *hate* it.

I just can't handle living at home any more. Susan, who's one of our crowd, is looking for someone to share a place. She recently came over from Ireland and has been staying with her brother. She works at Luton Airport and part-time in The Clarence. We find a maisonette to rent and move in November. It's a bit of a dump but we've got our own rooms and, best of all, I'm away from my family.

Susan and I get along okay. We're supposed to split the household bills, but she's always short of cash and I often end up paying for everything. I know she knows that I make myself sick. One day I cook leeks, mashed potatoes and a cheese sauce for us. I eat it, then go to the bathroom to weigh myself. God, I'm so heavy, I can't stand it. 'Right,' I think, sticking my fingers down my throat, 'you're going to bloody throw.' 'Enjoy yourself did you?' Susan says sarcastically as I come out of the bathroom. 'What do you mean?' I say, all innocence. 'You know what I mean,' she says, turning on her heel and going into her room.

I've changed jobs. I'm now assistant manager in Saxone shoe shop. I have to buy a size 14 skirt for work and I am mortified. I can hardly bring myself to jump on the scales now, but when I do they tip at over 11 stone. I've stopped having proper meals – I just eat all the time, grazing on a continuous stream of junk food. I feel tired and low; and bad thoughts about my body, my personality, my life jostle for space in my head. At least once a week my anger and desperation explode in a massive binge and vomit session. I usually plan to have it on my day off, when Susan is working at the airport; but sometimes, if I'm having a particularly bad week, I'm compelled to have a binge in the evening while she's at The Clarence.

On my day off I always go shopping in the morning. Into the trolley go things I normally buy – fat-free milk, low-fat spread, cheese, pasta. But I also bung in about 20 pounds' worth of the stuff I crave – gooey cakes, family bars of chocolate, biscuits, bread, butter, frozen pies and meals for one. I also buy things I don't like. I buy rice pudding – I *hate* rice pudding.

As soon as I get home I tip the shopping bags out on the kitchen counter and get the toaster going. I put some pasta on the hob, some roast potatoes and a frozen dinner in the oven, and a jacket potato in the microwave. I start ramming down a chocolate bar while I'm waiting for the toast; then I'll have an apple – something a bit healthy. I am surrounded by packets and cartons – mountains of food – and I feel excited, thrilled. The feeling is a bit like great sex, but I don't know that yet. Up pops the toast; quick, quick spread the butter, loads of it. Shove some more bread in the toaster – shove a couple of slices straight into my mouth. Ping! – the baked potato's ready. Tear open the microwave, flick the potato out onto the counter, slice it open and slather it with butter. It's really, really hot but I need to get it in me fast. I haven't got time to go over to the cupboard and get a plate out, let alone a knife and fork. I juggle it in my hands for a few seconds and then ram it into my mouth. I don't feel it burning my mouth, I don't even taste it; I don't taste any of it. Down the hatch it goes, into that industrial-sized waste-disposal unit – my stomach. I gulp large glasses of water to help it down. I'm not waiting for this cherry pie to defrost in the microwave – fee fi fo fum, look out tummy here it comes!

For several hours I sit on the floor with packets, cartons and wrappers around me. The world outside doesn't exist. All that I am aware of is the food that surrounds me on the kitchen floor; all I am thinking is how much I want this cake and how quickly I can shovel it in. Where's that water coming from? It's splashing onto the cake box. I put my hands up to my face – tears are pouring down my cheeks, but I feel nothing.

I eat until there is nothing left. It takes a couple of hours, but there is still a hole to fill. I peer into the empty fridge – there's a block of lard! How did I miss that? I gobble it down and swallow a load more water. My stomach is swollen and solid. I waddle to the bathroom and stare at myself in the mirror, long and hard. Look at my face; it's covered in food, my hands are sticky with bits of cake and my clothes look like a toddler's. I am repulsive.

Sometimes just seeing myself is enough to make me vomit. Otherwise I punch my fist into my stomach, open my mouth and heave; I'll punch and heave a couple more times and usually a medley of half-digested meals shoots out into the toilet. It doesn't always work though – it depends what I've eaten. Apples come up easily, but chocolate can be a pig, and if I've had a lot, it's harder to make myself vomit.

After one binge I dilute bleach with water and drink that. It burns my throat and doesn't even make me sick! I am desperate; panic isn't the word. I've consumed upwards of 15,000 calories and, if I don't get rid of the food, I am going to be huge. As a last resort I stick two fingers down my throat – my least favourite method. I retch, retch and retch again. Up come some pasta shells; they are whole, not even chewed. I taste them all over again. I stick my fingers down again and gag. Nothing happens. 'God,' I think to myself, 'I can't even make myself sick properly!' It's hard to breathe but I hold my fingers there and keep gagging. Big lumps of undigested food glob into the toilet bowl. I drink a pint of water; it helps the process, loosens things up. I'm sweating and getting palpitations. Dizzy dots play in front of my eyes. Bit by bit the rest of the food comes up. I can't taste the food any more, just bile. My eyes stream and the glands in my neck are swelling. I drink more water to wash out my stomach. Water is my marker; when only water comes out, I know my stomach is empty. Up it comes coloured pink with blood. I grazed my throat with my nail and didn't even notice.

The purging process takes about 20 minutes. I am hot, knackered, my eyes are little Chinese slits; my rings wedged on fingers puffed up like cocktail sausages, and my tummy hurts. I have no inkling that I am in danger of rupturing my stomach and killing myself within seconds – that people who binge and vomit are often found dead by the loo.

I brush my teeth – I don't know that this is the worst thing a bulimic can do, that I am rubbing acid from my stomach into the enamel. The acid is likely to erode tooth enamel and leave me with painfully sensitive, possibly even blackened, stumps. I wash my face and hands and climb into bed, where I spend the rest of the day. I rarely have a bath afterwards – I can't bear the thought of lying there looking down at my disgusting body.

———————

It's nearly Christmas. Martin and I have progressed from kissing to petting, and I am frightened by the spectre of sex. Martin always stops when I ask him to, but it seems easier to finish the relationship than to go on saying no. 'I don't want to go out with you any more,' I tell him one day. 'I'd rather we were just friends.' He refuses to talk to me.

Christmas comes. This year it's Granddad and Grandma's turn to come to Mum and Dad's house. I can't face the family, especially Granddad. I arrive for dinner, pig out, make my excuses and leave.

In January I don't send my brother a birthday card; and when Mum and Dad ring me one Sunday to tell me that their beloved Drummer has died, I can't be bothered to go round. Every night I go out straight from Saxone: I don't even bother to change. Still in my work clothes, I go to the pub and then on to The Hatters until three o'clock in the morning.

'Take this, it's really good,' says a girl in The Clarence one night. I look at her finger and on the tip is a tiny paper diamond starting to dissolve. I don't hesitate. I snatch it up and swallow it – anything for a crack. I just hope nobody tells Claire McCann – she'll put on her mum dress and give me a good telling-off. The pub is rocking and as the half tab of acid begins to take effect, my mouth stretches into a Cheshire Cat grin. I think my face will split, and every time somebody looks at me I laugh – even if they don't look I laugh. 'Let's go to The Hatters,' I say to Claire. 'Okay,' she says. 'Wait while I just go the toilet.' But I can't wait. I am fizzing. I grab Susan and sod off to The Hatters.

I am dancing to one of my favourite records, 'The Whole of the Moon' by The Waterboys, when Claire stomps in. Uh-oh, somebody's told her! 'What the fuck are you doing?' she yells. 'Why are you always trying to kill yourself?' Her mum dress is well and truly in position, and I am laughing my head off and spilling my pint of Guinness and black. It goes all over Susan's new cream jumper and I cackle even louder. 'You'll be the death of me,' says Claire as she grabs me, shoves me down the stairs and out into the night. 'I'm taking you home.' Helpless with the giggles, I let her.

Later I start to come down. I'm in bed: my body is floating, I can't feel my legs. I am paralysed from the waist down and terrified. I can't move, can't call out. 'I am never doing this again,' I think to myself, as my body starts to shake. No way.

I smoke cannabis and take speed though. Someone tells me that speed makes you lose weight because it quickens the metabolic rate so you don't want to eat, and you move all the time. I swallow what are known as 'bombs' – powdered amphetamine rolled up in rice paper. The first time I take it I am up for 48 hours. I close my eyes but bing! – they open like a cash-register. Somebody drops a dustbin lid and I start dancing, thinking it's a funky beat.

Chapter eleven

I am repulsed by myself – my size, my life, the person I've become. I'm out of control and I hate it. In the pub I drink myself stupid on strong cider, and one night I have 19 Tia Maria and Cokes. Alcohol makes the world fuzzier round the edges – a nicer, warmer place. The drugs help too. When I'm stoned on cannabis I feel so peaceful, I wouldn't care if somebody said the sky was going to fall in. If I take speed I am filled with energy – all I want to do is laugh, chat and dance. When I'm out of it I don't have to think about my problems, and I feel better about myself – briefly.

━━━━━━━━━━

I've been drinking Southern Comfort since I got home from work and I've already gone through half a bottle. I've got a bottle of painkillers too. And I'm pinching the hell out of my disgusting fat body, tipping the tablets out onto the carpet and toying with the idea of washing them down with the rest of the Southern Comfort and finishing it for good. Nobody seems to understand how awful it is for me to be this big. Every one tells me it's normal; but I've never been a size 14, never, and I am so angry with myself.

In desperation I ring the Samaritans. 'I want to die,' I say to a girl who tells me her name is Debbie. 'I've got some tablets and I'm going to take them.' I ramble drunkenly about how I want to kill myself because I'm too fat, and Debbie keeps me on the phone for a good three hours and talks me out of it. 'Count with me,' she says. 'Count the pills back into the bottle.' And I do it. 'I can send someone out to see you if you want,' says Debbie before she rings off. 'No!' I reply quickly, 'I'll be okay.' I can't have anyone seeing how fat I am!

I put down the phone, pick myself up off the floor, stagger through to the kitchen, slide open the cutlery drawer, and select the bread-knife to cut hell out of my stomach. I'm full of self-hatred and disgust – and it makes me want to hurt myself. The serrated steel edge bites into my skin and little bubbles of blood spring to the surface. But the knife isn't very sharp – it only scratches really. It doesn't even hurt. I pinch my blubbery tummy to make it hurt, to punish myself for being such a whale. I still can't feel anything. So then I get out the vinegar bottle and sprinkle it along the oozing horizontal wound. 'Fat bitch,' I say angrily, 'that'll teach you!'

Next morning I get up on what is to be the last day of my life. I can't cope with my miserable existence any more, and tonight I'm going to end it once and for all. Susan is staying the night at her boyfriend's, so I won't be disturbed. I put on my vile size 14 skirt. The hem's come down. It's only got to last a day, so I stick it up with Sellotape and go to the shop. I work hard, and mask my misery with a cheerful smile. Nobody must know there's anything wrong: I don't want anyone ruining my plans.

'Oh, fuck!' cries Susan. She's come back unexpectedly, heard the taps running and walked in on me in the bathroom. I am swaying by the basin. My fluffy white dressing gown is spattered with blood and a plastic razor is rattling against the plug hole in the flow from the taps. My wrists are slashed and bleeding but I feel nothing. 'Oh, *fuck!*' repeats Susan, as she turns and races to the front room to use the phone.

In a daze I stare at the wall. I don't remember coming into the bathroom, let alone picking up the razor, turning on the taps or slitting my wrists. Susan comes back muttering reassurances – Martin's coming over. She turns off the taps and guides me gently to my room, where she sits me on my bed. I don't protest. I am a zombie, one of the living dead. She dabs at my wrists with cotton wool. I watch but I don't feel – it's like the wounds belong to someone else. Susan applies gauze and thick brown plasters which she cuts from a roll. Martin arrives. 'Are you alright, Claire?' he asks. But I am dumb and cannot speak. I hear Martin and Susan talking – 'The wounds aren't too deep,' they say. 'Only bad scratches really' – but their voices sound far away. I lie down and slide into dreamless sleep.

———————————

'How are you, Claire?' Dr Pinto asks at my outpatient's appointment with him a few days later. 'Fine, thank you,' I say, pulling the sleeves of my long jumper over my hands. 'Let me see your arms,' he says. The penny drops. 'I am aware, Claire, that you have attempted to take your life,' he says flatly. 'Why did you do it?' 'It was an accident,' I reply. 'I don't believe it was an accident, Claire. I have been informed by your friends that you cut your wrists. They are very concerned for your health and we feel that it would be better for you to come into hospital right now. 'I'll be alright,' I insist, thinking, 'I'm too fat to go back into hospital. I can't possibly go back – a failed anorexic!'

A couple of weeks later I get back with Martin – God knows, I need somebody, and who else is going to put up with me? He knows I binge – Susan's told him; but he doesn't go on about it, or say anything about my abortive suicide attempt for that matter. I can't bring myself to talk about it. I want to block out the whole thing. I feel ashamed of what I did. I'm desperately unhappy, but I don't really want to *die*. I just don't know what goes on in my head sometimes. Perhaps I'm going crazy.

With Martin working behind the bar at The Clarence, I've an excuse to go to the pub every night and drink myself into a stupor. Martin doesn't seem to mind – in fact he lets me do what the hell I like – but then he's a bit of a pisshead himself. If he's had a few too many I notice he can get a bit stroppy with me; but then I'm such a mouthy cow, I probably deserve it.

I walk out of Saxone's after a row with the manager. In a torrent of bad language I tell him where he can stick his job. I hear myself shouting the harsh ugly words and squirm inside. This isn't me; this isn't how I want people to think of me. Back home I put on my Carpenters music, lie on my bed and burrow deeper and deeper into depression. Karen Carpenter is singing my pain.

I daydream about a life without pain, what I think of as 'my perfect world'. It's always the same fantasy. I'm walking in a field of long grass pushing a pram. The sun is shining, there's a feeling of warmth and love. I'm bending over the pram and smiling at the baby whose laughing face is turned up to me. That's my perfect world – someone to love who loves me back, unconditionally.

I've found the will-power to stop myself bingeing, thank God. I'm now on a starvation diet – nothing passes my lips but water, black tea and coffee and an apple a day. On the strength of a CV stuffed with lies about how I've cooked for banks in the past, I've landed a part-time job in a restaurant called Two's Company. I am a good cook though – anorexics usually are. I make all the savouries from scratch – lasagne, coronation chicken, and leek and potato soup, which is very popular and served with French bread topped with melted cheese. Mmm, my favourite! I don't eat any of it though – the smell is enough to satisfy me. My weight drops to 8 stone 10.

I'm back living with Mum and Dad. I don't like it, but I've no choice. Susan's gone home to Ireland, leaving me with a stack of bills and unable to keep on the maisonette. At least my brother Michael's moved out of home, so I can have his old room and don't have to share with my sister.

'I've got something I want to ask you,' Martin keeps saying. 'Well ask me then,' I say. 'No, I'll do it later,' he says and changes the subject. I've an idea what he wants to ask me, but I'm not letting on. He dithers all week until Saturday. We're in Tesco. 'I've got something to ask you,' he starts again. 'Just ask me, Martin,' I say, bored now. 'No, not here,' he says. 'Just ask,' I say, queuing for cigarettes. 'Will you marry me?' he stutters. There, he's said it – no bended knee, no flowers, no champagne, no ring even! 'Yeah,' I say, 'course. Now let's go to the pub.'

I don't love Martin, but he can give me the baby I want so badly – my perfect world. And, if I marry him, I won't have to live at home any more. The tension between my family and me is unbearable, and I can't maintain my starvation diet with Mum and Dad on the warpath. 'Martin and I are getting engaged,' I announce. There's no ceremony, no formal asking for my hand; I don't even bother to invite Martin round when I tell Mum and Dad. They've met him a couple of times and I don't think they're too impressed, but they know better than to say anything.

I buy my own engagement ring. It's a single diamond set in gold and costs £60 from F. Hinds. I'm earning more money now: I've given up my part-time job at Two's Company for a full-time position at Woolworths. 'That's lovely,' says Martin when I show him the ring. 'I'll pay you back when I can.' We plan to marry the following May and I tell Martin I want to start a family straight away. I've picked out and paid for my wedding dress in a shop called Mignonette. It's got short ruched sleeves, a tight bodice and a long frothy train. It's gorgeous – well, I think so. Martin keeps asking me what it's like but I'm not telling – it's supposed to be bad luck.

One Friday I breeze out of Woolworths at the end of the day and walk past the Nat West Bank, and there is a dress like mine in a wedding display to promote loans. I shiver and walk on quickly, convinced it's an omen.

Later that night, my dream of a perfect world lies in tatters. For the first time one of Martin's moods boils over into uncontrollable rage. He hits me, hard. I don't even know what I'm supposed to have done. Perhaps it's because I won't have sex with him, perhaps it's because we've both been drinking, perhaps it's just because I'm me.

'Dear Martin,' I write next day, stopping to re-examine the livid set of bruises circling my upper arm. 'I've always said that if any guy ever lays one finger on me, they're gone – so goodbye. From Claire.' I put the letter in an envelope with the engagement ring which he still hasn't paid me for, and post it on my way to work. I walk past my wedding dress in Nat West's window and start to cry. First Granddad abuses me, and now Martin. Why me? What's wrong with me?

Chapter twelve

'Claire,' says Mum hesitantly, 'I was cleaning your room and I found this.' 'What?' I say, sitting up in bed and rubbing the sleep from my eyes. It's first thing in the morning; I got in late last night and I am having a lie in because it's Claire McCann's 21st birthday party tonight.

Mum's holding a battered shorthand notebook. Hang on a minute, it's one of mine! I look at her as if to say, 'What the hell are you doing with that?' 'Claire,' says Mum, her voice tight with anxiety, 'it says in here that you were sexually abused by one of the family. Who was it?' The bed seems to have been whisked away beneath me; the room spins. I can feel the colour drain from my face and I start to sweat. 'Was it when you were younger, when you and Michael were playing games?' says Mum, kneeling by the bed. 'No,' I shake my head. 'Was it Dad?' she asks, searching my face. 'No,' I say, my mind racing. I'm going to have to tell her. It's all going to come out and then I'll split up the family. 'Claire, what's gone on, what's happened? You've got to tell me who it was,' she begs, her voice breaking. I look at Mum; she's distraught, shocked to the core by what she's read, desperate to know, desperate to make things alright again. 'It was Granddad,' I whisper, and start to howl like a little girl.

'Oh!' cries Mum, putting her arms round me. 'Why didn't you tell us, Claire?' 'I couldn't,' I reply, forcing out the words between big sobs. 'I didn't think you'd believe me. I didn't want to break up the family. Don't tell anybody, please,' I say, feeling sick, ashamed and desperate that no one else should find out. 'I'm going to have to tell Dad, Claire,' she says. Shakily, she stands up, wipes her eyes and goes downstairs to do so. I lie back on the pillows. God, I need a cigarette.

———————

'I'm going to kill him, I'm going to bloody kill him!' shouts Dad, clenching and unclenching his fists. Dad's boiling with a terrible temper. He rarely gets like this but when he does he can do serious damage. We're in the kitchen. I'm smoking. Things must be bad: I'm not allowed to smoke indoors because of Lisa's asthma. 'No, Dad,' I beg, 'please, don't!' 'No, John,' says Mum, looking scared: she knows what he's like when he flies off the handle. She doesn't care about Granddad, she's thinking about Dad. 'Promise you won't Dad,' I insist. 'Granddad's sorry, he's really sorry.' What I've dreaded is happening – and it's all my fault. 'Okay,' says Dad, calming down a little, 'I promise I won't hurt him, but I've got to go and see him.' He bolts out of the back-door leaving Mum pacing the floor and muttering, 'I would have trusted him with my kids' lives.' I draw heavily on my cigarette. I'm never going to forget this day as long as I live.

I go through the motions that afternoon. I'm drained: my mind keeps turning to Mum and Dad knowing and my gorge begins to rise. I'm dirty, I'm a freak. I can't bear the thought of people knowing, and I've made Mum and Dad promise not to tell another soul. I go into town and buy Claire a bracelet for her birthday. Then I call in at the house my brother Michael shares with his friend Kevin. Elaine, Michael's new girlfriend, is there too and it's a relief to sit around in Michael's room, watching him play games on the computer, and talking about nothing in particular. The phone goes and Michael runs downstairs to answer it.

'Claire,' calls Michael from the living room. 'Yeah,' I reply, walking to the top of the stairs. 'Can you come down here a minute?' I go downstairs, thinking, 'He's made us all a coffee and needs a hand carrying it up.' I walk into the front room and my brother is standing in the middle of the room with tears in his eyes. 'Claire,' he says, pulling me towards him, 'I am so so sorry. I was starting to hate you, I didn't understand you.' 'What?' I say, confused and stiff in his arms. 'Mum and Dad have told me,' he says. I pull away from him, open my mouth and scream, 'No!' I asked them not to tell; they promised. I can't stop screaming. I scream the scream of someone being murdered, the sort of scream that you imagine could bring buildings tumbling down. I hear Elaine and Kevin clattering down the stairs. 'Watch her, don't let her go anywhere!' shouts Michael to them. 'Where are you going?' I cry. 'I'm going to kill him!' he spits with venom. 'You can't!' I'm yelling. 'Please, Michael, don't!' But he runs out of the house, jumps into his car and screeches away from the kerb.

Back home, I block out what's happened. It's been a terrible day, but it's my best friend's party tonight and I'm going to try to have a good time. On goes the electric-blue eyeliner and a red off-the-shoulder top. It's a warm May evening and we all have a lot to drink. Claire and I are beginning to sway. Putting her arms round me and giving me a kiss, she slurs, 'You're my bestest-ever friend.'

Chapter thirteen

'Those blokes are staring at us,' says Lisa in an excited whisper. It's the first night of our holiday in Rhodes. Deciding I need cheering up, Mum and Dad have brought us to a place called Reni Koskinou for a couple of weeks. We're staying at the Hotel Paradise, and it's beautiful – all white paint and great archways laden with pink bougainvillaea. I can see two guys looking across the restaurant at us. One is dark and unattractive, the other is muscular with blond hair, a broad back and a golden tan. But I'm not the least bit interested – I've had enough of men.

'Hi, I'm Roy and this is Malcolm,' the blond one says in a thick Birmingham accent. We're sitting by the pool after our meal, and Dad asks them to join us. 'We know Rhodes quite well now,' they say, 'so any time you girls want to go out, let us know.'

That first week I lounge round the pool in my bikini. I look fat in my bikini but I want to get as brown as possible – you look thinner when you're brown, don't you? People insist that I'm not overweight, but I don't care what they say. I'm used to being thin and angular, used to my clothes flapping off me like I'm a wire coat-hanger. I loathe my rounded womanly shape; I hate the way the seams of my clothes sit snugly against my skin. I'm being careful about what I eat, but it's not hard as I hate foreign food – I'm not one for trying new things – and most of the dishes on the salad bar are swamped in yukky dressing.

Roy and Malcolm keep coming over and sitting with us by the pool. They buy us drinks. 'They seem very nice lads,' says Mum.

Since Mum and Dad found out about the abuse we've been getting on better. Now they know what I've been through, they're not so hard on me. They don't go on so much about my eating, or my smoking for that matter. I'm not glad they know though. I hate it. I cringe when I think of it. When they try to speak to me about it I clam up: 'Don't wanna talk about it,' I say through clenched teeth and walk out. I need Mum and Dad though, more than ever. Lately, I've been feeling insecure and vulnerable, like a little child. I keep thinking, 'What if Mum and Dad die, what'll happen to me?' I find myself in tears at the thought of being without them.

After a week, Roy and Malcolm ask Lisa and me if we'd like to go into the nearby town of Faliraki. Fancying a change of scene, we say yes. I don't dress up; I'm not interested in impressing them. Faliraki is a buzzing place. We go to a few bars for a few drinks and have quite a giggle. Roy's 32 and he's a DJ at a club in Swindon. It turns out he used to work at a nightclub in Luton. 'Small world, isn't it?' we both say. In one of the bars there's an Oldham football scarf hanging up – it reminds me of Martin. Roy tries to hold my hand, but I pull it away.

Mum, Dad and Lisa have gone on a day-trip, leaving me to toast myself by the pool. Roy saunters over. 'Come out with me tonight,' he says. He *is* nice, and very good-looking. Why not?

We go round some of the bars in Faliraki, and then to a disco in a hotel. We dance to 'The Whole of the Moon' by The Waterboys. I tell him about Martin, and he talks about his brother who died last year after an illness. It's sad, and I find myself telling Roy how I've been ill with anorexia and spent some time in hospital. He's really sympathetic. 'It must have been awful,' he says, adding, 'you've got a lovely figure now.'

We get back to the hotel at midnight, walk past the pool and down the steps to the private beach. We talk some more, and watch a yacht moored off the beach rock as the rich Greek who owns it has his way with yet another young English girl. The insects whir and a breeze lifts my flarey short skirt. Some time later we look up to see the stars being sucked away by the sun – it's dawn; we've been talking for six hours! 'God, I'd better go,' I say. 'Mum and Dad'll go mad if they find out I've been out all night!' I brush the sand away from my skirt and Roy takes my hand and lifts me to my feet. I feel so close to him. Hand in hand we walk up the steps and past the pool. Then he picks me up and kisses me and my stomach flutters with happiness. It never felt like this with Martin.

Roy's arranged to take me out on the motorbike he's hired. Dad's forbidden me to go on motorbikes, so we're going to have to be sneaky. 'I'm going out with Roy for the day,' I say to my parents, and what a day it turns out to be. It's my first time on a motorbike, and we've no helmets or protective clothing. We zoom into the mountains to find the Valley of the Butterflies. It should take about an hour but we get lost. It doesn't matter – we're having such a great time. Higher and higher we climb and at one point we think we can see Turkey. Our bums get sore, so we stop every now and again by the side of the road to swig water from a bottle and share a cigarette.

By the time we get back to the hotel, we're covered from head-to-toe in dust from the road. It's everywhere – on our clothes, in our hair, our mouths, our shoes. We're late for our evening meal but we can't go into the restaurant, the state we're in. So we go back to Roy's room to tidy ourselves up. 'Jump in the shower,' says Roy. I wash as quickly as I can. Mum and Dad are going to kill me if they find out I've been on a motorbike. I've got to clean myself up and get to the restaurant, quick.

Swiftly, I wind a small white towel round my hair and wrap a larger one round my body. As I charge out of the bathroom, Roy catches me in his arms. Very gently he takes the towel from my head and shakes down my hair. Then without a word he unwraps the towel from around my body. And it doesn't bother me. I'm standing there completely naked and it doesn't bother me one bit. I know it's going to happen and I want it to happen. As Roy picks me up in his arms and lays me on the bed I send up a little prayer: 'Oh God, please let me know what it's like to feel normal. Please let it be nice.' And it is.

———————————

'What would you do if you were pregnant?' says Roy. It's his last day and I am heartbroken. 'I don't know,' I reply; the thought hasn't even crossed my mind. All I can think about is that I've got to get him alone before he leaves – I want to make love to him all the time. 'I wouldn't support you,' he says. But I'm so in love, I don't care. If Roy told me to jump off a cliff I would.

Back in England, Roy and I speak on the phone and I send him letters. I even record a load of soppy love songs onto a tape and send it to him. Roy says he's coming to see me, but he hasn't been able to get away yet. At Woolworths our delivery truck comes in from Swindon – I'm thinking about hiding in the back of it and going to surprise him. 'He's only after the five Fs, Claire,' warns my friend Catherina who works on the sweet counter, 'find 'em, feel 'em, fool 'em, fuck 'em, forget 'em.' But I don't believe her.

Eventually Roy does come to Luton. I'm over-joyed to see him; but a bit dismayed that Malcolm's with him. 'I've got something for you,' says Roy. It's the single 'The Whole of the Moon': our song. On it he's written 'Claire, Remember Rhodes 1990, Roy. XXX'. We spend the evening at a few pubs and then Roy and Malcolm say they've got to get back. I'm gutted: I've arranged for us to stay at a friend's house so Roy and I can have sex. 'Never mind, I'll be back again soon,' says Roy, kissing me goodbye. But Catherina was right: he ignores my letters and refuses to take my phone calls.

Chapter fourteen

Catherina's a laughing girl from County Wexford. Her exotic dark looks led me to think that she might be half-Portuguese at first, but she's Irish through and through. She lives with her boyfriend, Daffy, who's a carpenter. They left Ireland a year ago and came to England to seek work. Catherina knows that I've had anorexia. Now it's behind me, I don't mind talking about it. We go out one dinner-time and I suggest we have a go on the electronic weighing scales in Boots. Catherina goes first. She weighs 10 stone. I'm 8 stone 13, and I think that's quite big. It's less than Catherina, but so it should be; I'm a different build. 'That's quite low,' says Catherina, looking alarmed. 'Promise me you won't get sick again.' 'I won't,' I say and I mean it; I can't imagine going back to being the poor calorie-obsessed creature that I was before I went into hospital.

Trouble is, I'm heartbroken over Roy. My virtually non-existent self-esteem has been dealt a fatal blow and I hate myself. I have my shoulder-length hair viciously cropped like a boy's and dye it bright blonde.

It doesn't make me like myself any more though; I am still deeply unhappy with the way I am. I lose my appetite and the pounds begin to slip away. Mum and Dad start commenting on my weight again – I don't know what they're on about. I'm not even thinking about food; I'm certainly not dieting or taking laxatives.

It's November and Catherina and I have both left Woolworths: she's working at Evans, the clothes shop and I'm working for Radio Rentals. My official title is 'sales receptionist' and I rent out televisions, videos and washing machines. I have a uniform – a navy skirt, a blue and white striped blouse, a red dotted bow tie and a navy jacket. I love the job and think I'm getting over Roy at long last. There is a fly in my ointment though, a tall skinny one called Gaynor. She's another sales receptionist and I'm jealous of her. She weighs 8 stone – I know because I've asked her – but she eats like a horse. She's lovely-looking too, with powder-blue eyes and blonde hair. 'I want to be the size of Gaynor,' I think to myself, 'but I wouldn't look that skinny if I was 8 stone so I'll have to get below it.'

The run-up to Christmas is always my panic-time anyway. I start to cut back, to compensate for all the food I know I'm going to eat on Christmas Day. This will be the first Christmas since Mum and Dad found out about Granddad, the first when we won't all be together as a family. Catherina and Daffy are going home to Ireland over the holiday period and they've asked me to house-sit. I'm pleased; it takes the pressure off me a bit. I'm literally only going home for Christmas dinner.

Christmas Day isn't too bad. As usual I let myself eat as much as I want; as usual I am ridden with guilt. Grandma pops in to give us presents. Socks for

Michael, tights for Lisa and me. The gift tags say 'Love from Grandma'; there's no mention of Granddad. It's strange to think that none of us has set foot in Grandma and Granddad's house since May, when everything came out. Sometimes I wonder how I'd feel going back into that house, seeing him – but I try not to think about it too much.

My New Year's resolution in January 1991 is, as usual, to lose a few pounds. As my work skirt begins to swing off me, Mum starts going on at me and my colleagues at Radio Rentals notice. 'Why have you got such a low opinion of yourself?' asks one of the girls at work, when I make some comment about being ugly. 'You're a really nice girl.' 'Yes,' chimes in someone else, 'and you never eat anything and you're getting really thin.' 'I do eat,' I protest, more out of habit than anything.

I transfer to the Radio Rentals shop in Dunstable which is run by Jan. In her early 30s, Jan has a bright and bubbly personality. 'Hello darlin',' she always calls out in her sing-song voice. She's got short, bleached-blonde hair too, and sometimes the customers ask if we are sisters. She's really enthusiastic about sales. When the phone goes she grabs it and gabbles 'GoodmorningRadioRentals, JanspeakinghowcanIhelpyou?' which makes me laugh. I've got down to 8 stone; but, as I say, I've got to be less than that to look as skinny as Gaynor. Plus summer's coming, and I want to look nice in all those skimpy clothes. More often than not I don't eat anything during the day and Jan, a self-confessed crisp fanatic, is starting to worry.

I'll have a meal in the evening if I'm staying in, but I'm going out a lot. I've started singing at karaoke nights in local pubs, and things are so exciting – I've won the first heat in a karaoke competition! I think I've found my vocation: I want to be a singer.

I'm really nervous: The Heights is a massive pub, the place is packed for the semi-final of the karaoke competition and loads of people from Radio Rentals have come to watch me. I'm wearing black leggings, and notice that the material is bagging about my thighs. I'm 7 stone 6. Mum got rid of the scales long ago, but I weigh myself at Catherina's. I'm feeling a bit shaky. I ask if I can have a stool to sit on. Sitting in the middle of the pub I gulp at the faces staring at me in silence, and launch into 'Yesterday Once More' by The Carpenters. For a few fleeting minutes I am transported to a different world. I *am* Karen Carpenter, and this isn't a pub – it's the London Palladium. I concentrate on performing for the audience, and for a brief period I escape my awful life. When I finish the pub erupts in cheers, claps and screams. 'You were brilliant!' people say as I walk back to my place. 'You sound just like Karen Carpenter.' 'Wow!' I think, 'what an honour.'

I can hear the compere calling out my name. Eventually his words sink into my brain. They mean me! I can't have won, can I? I don't believe it. I've won! Urged to my feet by my friends I walk towards the compere in a daze. Catherina is crying and all around me people are standing on chairs and tables, clapping, cheering and stamping their feet. This is my 15 minutes of fame. I'm pulled aside by a woman from the local radio station and collared by a journalist and his photographer who pops flash-bulbs in my face. 'Claire Carpenter!' screams the headline in the local newspaper.

CHAPTER FOURTEEN

The final of the karaoke competition is being held at a nightclub in Milton Keynes, not far from Jan's house. I'm changing for the competition in her spare room, when she walks in. 'Oh, my God!' says Jan, her hand whizzing up to her mouth, 'there's nothing of you!' In my bra and knickers, I am hoisting up a pair of black ski pants. 'Claire, you've got to do something; you're just skin and bone!' Jan's really upset; in fact she starts crying. I'm shocked. I don't know what she's talking about. What a fuss. I'm not thin at all. Quickly I cover myself up with my black sleeveless waistcoat. Jan's grabbing hold of my arms, feeling my waist. She's muttering about my stick-like arms and saying, 'You can't wear that, it looks horrendous! Perhaps I've got something you can wear.' Jan's clothes match her personality: she wears loud pink and purple jackets with big shoulder-pads. She's a size 10 with big boobs and her clothes just hang off me. I have to wear my original outfit: it's okay – at least it covers my huge bum.

I don't win the competition – I can hardly catch my breath, let alone sing. 'Does Claire have cancer or AIDS or something?' someone asks one of my friends.

As summer ends the district managers, Linda Jennart and Cathy Johnson, come into Radio Rentals to talk to me about my weight. 'You have to get help,' they say. 'But I am eating,' I protest. I can't understand it. It's not like I'm not eating. Okay, I'm not tucking into pizza or chips, but I'm not on my slice-of-cheese-and-bread-roll-a-day diet. I am pretty much sticking to food I feel safe with, like egg in salad cream sandwiches and pasta. I'm troubled by people going on at me all the time and my thoughts are confused. I'm determined not to give in and eat more just because people say I should. I'm also getting into the laxatives again – after all, if everyone thinks I'm doing something wrong, I might as well go the whole hog.

'Every time I come into the shop, you look thinner,' says Linda. 'We need to get you to the doctor's.' I agree because I don't want to lose my job. I'm scared though; I don't want to go back into hospital.

Just before Linda comes to collect me, I go up to my room, peel back the bedroom carpet where I've hidden my laxatives and shovel down a handful. It makes me feel a little calmer, a bit safer.

Dr O'Donnell isn't on duty so we see another doctor who refers me straight back to the Faringdon Wing. A week later I see Dr Pereira, the Registrar under Dr Pinto, and a community psychiatric nurse called Ruby. Dr Pereira is an Indian in his mid-30s who can't say his Vs. I like him. He has a special interest in people with eating problems, and seems to want to listen and take his time with me.

Ruby is a large coffee-coloured lady with cropped black hair. She sits and looks stern while Dr Pereira asks me a bunch of questions in his gentle considered manner. He gets me to draw a picture of myself. I pick up a pen and sketch my huge chipmunk cheeks, big bloated belly and huge backside. 'Mmm,' says Dr Pereira, thoughtfully, 'you have a wery distorted body image.' At the end of the consultation Dr Pereira tells me that Ruby will be monitoring my weight. I'll see her once a week for half an hour at a place called Beacon House, a short walk from Radio Rentals.

Every week it's the same. 'Let's weigh you, shall we?' Ruby says. 'I don't want to be weighed,' I reply.

'Why do you say this every week? You know you have to be weighed,' Ruby retorts, her Caribbean voice lilting upwards. I step on the scales, cringing. 'Good, you've gained a little weight,' Ruby says, or more usually, 'Claire, you've lost weight.' Then she draws me a graph which indicates how many pounds she wants me to put on, and which I will throw away as soon as I leave Beacon House. She asks me for my food diary, which I won't have. Each day I am supposed to write down what I eat and how I feel about it, but I never do. 'How many times do I have to tell you, you must keep your food diary?' Ruby says, wagging one of her gold-varnished fingernails in my direction. Then before the session ends she asks me about my week. I tell her that I feel bad about an argument I've had with Mum and Dad, or this, that or the other. 'Bad bad bad bad bad,' Ruby shrieks, 'That's all I hear. Why do you feel so bad? Why are you always putting yourself down? Tell me something nice about yourself.' There's always a deathly silence.

Chapter fifteen

'Hiya!' It's Andy Beeken. He used to work at British Home Stores, until he left to be a storeman at LTH Electronics. We bump into each other in the street outside Radio Rentals. God, he's changed. His face is the same, and his brown hair is still short and spiky but he's filled out. He used to be skinny but now he's all manly-looking; his back is really broad – I like broad backs. 'Where are you off to then?' I ask, looking at his holdall. 'To the pool,' he says. 'I've started swimming every Tuesday.' 'I'll go with you next week,' I reply. 'I could do with the exercise.' 'Okay,' says Andy, 'you're on.'

Andy's a right laugh. When he was at British Home Stores he sat in a bath of custard in his swimming trunks to raise money for Comic Relief. And I'll never forget the time when Claire McCann, Rosaleen, Andy and I raced each other round the stockroom wearing mannequin wigs. I like Andy but I don't think of him as a prospective boyfriend: I don't imagine for a minute that he'd want me as his girlfriend.

I'm looking forward to Tuesday, but I'm worried Andy'll think I'm fat. I'm 7 stone 10, but after taking laxatives for a few days I get down to 7½. In the changing-room I slip into my green and white striped swimming costume – the stripes go downwards, it's more slimming. I stare at myself in the mirror and am temporarily reassured to see that my chest bones are poking through my skin, my pelvic bones are protruding and my stomach is concave.

'You've got a great figure,' says Andy in the pool. 'You're really slim.' I am crushed: with my warped self-perception, slim equals fat. Everybody else has been telling me that I'm really underweight and looking emaciated; well, they obviously don't know what I look like under my clothes. Andy's seeing me in my swimming costume and he doesn't think I'm emaciated – obviously I look bigger out of my clothes than in. It doesn't occur to me that it's a chat-up line; I don't imagine that anybody wants to chat me up.

But Andy keeps ringing me and we go out. After three weeks he takes me to see *JFK* at The Point cinema complex in Milton Keynes. It's an amazing film, and as he drives me home we chatter away about who we think shot JFK. He pulls up outside Mum and Dad's, and kisses me for the first time. There are no fireworks or marching bands, but I am pleased. I've been liking Andy more and more and have been unsure whether we were boyfriend and girlfriend or just friends. The kiss makes it official.

———————

'I don't really want anything to eat,' I say to Andy. We're sitting in his bedroom and he's showing me his weights. He lives with his mum and stepfather.

He has a sister called Diane, who's a year younger than me, and an older brother. I feel comfortable at Andy's, partly because his mum loves animals and it's like animal kingdom round there. There are fish and rabbits, Henry and Wilma the dogs, and the cats, Samson, Humphrey and Burbank. His mum has produced a plate of sandwiches made with processed cheese squares, lettuce, tomato, cucumber and sweetcorn on white bread. 'Go on,' says Andy, 'have a sandwich.' 'No,' I say, 'I'm getting a bit too big. I don't want anything, really.'

Andy remembers that I was ill when I worked at British Home Stores and we talk a little about it. I feel comfortable enough to tell him that I still have to see a community psychiatric nurse now. 'You are a bit skinny, actually,' says Andy. 'Bloody hell,' I think to myself, 'he said I was slim before.' People contradict themselves all the time; from now on I'm just going to be true to what I believe – that I'm too fat.

Andy is shy; he's a year older than me but he hasn't had many girlfriends. We kiss and that's about it – which suits me. At the beginning of 1992 I sense that Andy wants to get more serious. The one thing I am *not* is naive – I know men like to have sex. I liked sex once – with Roy. But after the disastrous way that relationship ended, I'm back to square one – to me sex means being used and abused.

I'm going to have to come straight out with it – tell Andy why I'm funny about sex. I don't want to, but sex is more frightening. 'Andy,' I begin one day when we are sitting in his bedroom, 'sex is a bit of a problem for me.' I take a deep breath. 'You see, I was abused by my granddad when I was younger. So I don't want you to take it personally if I pull away from you sometimes.' Andy doesn't know what to say. I can see he's shocked. After a few moments, he pulls himself together and says, 'It doesn't matter Claire; I'll wait as long as it takes.'

'They're running a book on us at work,' laughs Andy. We're driving back to Luton after having a pizza with Cathy Johnson and her boyfriend. We've had a couple of drinks and a few laughs and it's been a nice evening. 'What do you mean?' I ask him. 'They reckon we'll get engaged,' he says, smiling sideways at me. I don't know what to say, but I know I like Andy a lot. The feelings I have for him are different to those that I had for Roy, but I think I must have confused lust with love. 'What do you reckon then?' he asks. 'What?' I say. 'Well,' he replies, pulling up at my house, putting on the handbrake and turning to me. 'Shall we prove them right? Shall we get engaged?' I'm thrilled. 'That would be great,' I say, kissing him.

Andy's really nervous; we both are. We keep looking at one another and bursting into giggles. He's planning to tell Mum and Dad over Sunday dinner. 'Ding, ding': the clock in the living room chimes two o'clock. It sounds prophetic and Andy and I start laughing all over again. 'Dinner's ready!' shouts Dad from the kitchen where he's been carving the roast and Mum's been straining the vegetables. 'Here goes,' I mouth at Andy, as we go through to the kitchen.

We sit at the table and Andy says nothing about getting engaged. We eat chicken, stuffing and roast potatoes. Still Andy's lips are sealed. Mum brings out the dessert. I think Andy's lost his nerve. Chit chat chit – we talk about everything under the sun and then somehow the subject of marriage comes up. Andy clears his throat and says in a tight voice, 'Er, how would you feel about me and Claire getting married?' There's a few seconds' silence and then Mum and Dad both speak at once. 'That's wonderful!' exclaims Mum. 'It's a bit bloody soon isn't it?' says Dad, before he can stop himself. I'm not surprised, but I know Mum'll talk him round. 'No, it's not,' says Mum, giving Dad one of her looks. 'It's great news!'

A week later Andy and I are at Mill Rythe, a holiday centre on Hayling Island where the staff are called Team Stars. We wondered why the holiday was so cheap, and now we know – it's OAP week! Wherever you look there's someone singing 'Hello, Dolly!', doing the foxtrot or playing bingo. Andy and I don't care though, we think it's a giggle; and we've got almost exclusive use of the swimming pools, the sauna, the Jacuzzi and the bicycles, because everybody else is so elderly. Mill Rythe is set in beautiful countryside. There are rolling fields, streams crossed by little bridges, and views over the sea. We've booked a room in the apartment block, not a chalet, because the rooms are nicer and you get a TV. We had to pay a bit extra, but even so the holiday's only costing us £75 each which includes three meals a day. I tuck in, but I find I need Andy's constant reassurance. 'Do you think I'm fat?' I ask. 'Am I putting on weight?'

One evening Andy orders a bottle of Asti Spumante for us to have with our meal. He fills our glasses and then bobs down on to one knee. 'Claire, will you marry me?' he grins. 'Yes,' I say, laughing and enjoying the looks of all the other people in the restaurant, 'I'll marry you.' He gets out a little square blue box. I know it contains the diamond cluster we chose together at H. Samuel last week. He slips the ring on my finger and it's official – we're engaged.

———

Back from Hayling Island I feel huge. I've been eating three heavy meals a day. I've got an outpatient's appointment at the hospital and I know they'll weigh me. I'm really scared to know how much I've put on. When Ruby weighed me two weeks ago I was 8 stone. 'I hope I'm the same,' I think, climbing onto the scales with a heavy heart. Up shoots the needle – 8 stone 11: I've put on 11 pounds! I'm on a diet – I can't be a fat bride!

We fix the wedding date and book St John the Apostle Catholic church for the ceremony, and the hall next door for the reception. Mum and I go looking for my wedding dress. I flick through the huge meringues of dresses hanging in rows in Mignonette – creams, whites, roses, beads, frills and puffs. I pull one out. I think I've found the perfect dress. 'That one,' I say to the assistant. 'Can I try that one, please?' The assistant unhooks it from the rail and carries the creation before her like a trophy into the fitting-room. I follow and she swishes the curtains closed behind me. I look at the vision before me hanging on the padded coat-hanger: it's off-white with big puffed sleeves, a V-shaped bodice which goes into a point at the front – very slimming – and an endless train. It's a bit like Princess Diana's dress and I love it. They only have a size 12 – I hope it fits.

With a small smile of satisfaction I see the dress doesn't just fit; it's miles too big. The assistant steps in to zip me up and there are bunches of material where a body should be. 'You're too skinny,' says

Mum, disapprovingly. 'You need a size 10,' says the assistant, adding, 'If you order it now, you'll get it in January.' It's £650 and Mum pays. I'm going to have to be really careful now. The saga of the lemon bridesmaid dress I wore to Katrina-up-the-road's wedding remains ingrained in my mind. I begin to panic in case history repeats itself. I can't put on an ounce; in fact, I think I'll lose a few more pounds to be on the safe side.

I strike on the idea of becoming a blood donor. After all, a pint bag of blood probably weighs about the same as a 2-pound bag of sugar, doesn't it? 'Are you sure you're 8 stone?' asks the nurse. 'I'm 8 stone 1 to be precise,' I lie. You have to be at least 8 stone to give blood, but luckily the nurse seems to take me at my word. I pass the prick test for anaemia and now the nurse is trying in vain to raise a vein. It takes a few minutes but eventually the needle is inserted and I watch the red fat shooting through the clear tube into a bag above the bed. It's very gratifying – until I pass out.

I come round to find that the needle's been whisked out of my arm and the bag's only an inch full. A doctor is at my bedside. 'I think you need your blood more than we do,' she smiles, adding, 'now eat these, and don't move for at least half an hour.' She hands me a glass of orange juice and not one, but four biscuits! I have no choice but to smile sweetly and eat them. Inside, I'm fuming.

Andy and I have found the house of our dreams. Built in the 1930s, it has two bedrooms, a big front room and adjoining dining room, the same size. The kitchen leads on to a little garden, but it's the bath-room which sells it to me. It's huge, with a vanity unit, bath and shower. There is no off-road parking, but it doesn't really matter as Andy's selling his car so we'll have a small deposit to put down.

We make an offer. It's accepted and we take out a joint mortgage, but there's no question of us mov-ing in and living together. Mum and Dad are anti-sex before marriage, end of story. I don't mind too much – it puts off the sex thing a bit longer. And Mum and Dad have no objections to us staying there on a Friday and Saturday night – they think I sleep on the blow-up double Lilo and Andy's in the single bed in the spare room. In fact we snuggle up togeth-er on the Lilo, and if my parents come over on a Sunday morning Andy races into the spare room, rumples the bedclothes and dents the pillows. We don't *do* anything, but Mum and Dad would never believe us!

We have little furniture – a two-seater settee that somebody gave us and a cooker which I bought for a tenner. After work on a Friday I'll buy something nice for tea, and cook while Andy potters in the garden. Andy brings his portable colour TV from home and we'll watch a bit of telly and talk about the wedding and our plans for the house – Andy's going to make the spare room into a mini-gym.

'Hello Kim,' I say as my old friend and colleague from British Home Stores rushes up to me in the town centre when I'm out shopping. I haven't seen her in ages. 'Do you remember Veronica?' she says. I nod, thinking back to the shy girl who worked on

Saturdays at BHS. 'Well,' continues Kim, 'she's really ill, Claire. She's lost loads of weight. Will you go in and see her?' 'Course I will, Kim,' I say. I walk into BHS, towards Ladies Fashions where Veronica is working. I can't believe the change: she used to be a big girl, now she's a little matchstick person.

'Hi, Veronica,' I say, 'do you remember me?' 'Yes,' she says, her head twitching nervously to one side as a deep blush spreads over her face. I try to talk generally at first, but it's like pulling teeth. I get straight to the point. 'I think you've got a problem haven't you?' I say. 'No,' she says quietly. I try a different tack. 'Do you remember when I worked here and went into hospital?' I say. 'Yes,' she whispers, looking at her feet. Her head jerks to one side again. 'I do understand, I know what it's like. You don't have to be frightened of telling me you've got a problem,' I say, adding, 'We could meet up and have a chat if you like?' I write my number on an old bus ticket and hand it to her.

'Claire, Veronica's on the phone,' calls Mum. I come flying down the stairs. 'Hi, Veronica,' I say. 'Can we still meet for a chat?' asks Veronica, getting straight to the point. 'Sure, when?' I reply. Quickly we make arrangements to meet the following week – I can tell she wants to get off the phone. Perhaps her mum told her to ring.

It's pissing down with rain and I shelter in the doorway of British Home Stores. Veronica is late. I wonder if she's going to turn up. I'll give her another 10 minutes. Then I see her walking towards me from the Arndale Centre. She's wearing a brown leather jacket and a pair of trousers way too big. Her head is bowed against the rain. As she draws nearer and focuses on me I can see her sad little pinched face under its cap of bright hair, and I think to myself, 'She's in a sorry state.'

We go to The Clarence. She gets the drinks, and comes back with my Diet Coke and, I'm surprised to see, half a lager for herself. I ask all the questions, and she isn't very forthcoming. I gather that her father died recently and that she has an over-riding feeling that she is fat. 'I feel big,' she says repeatedly, 'and if I eat anything I make myself sick.' I feel so badly for her. She's such a lovely girl; I want to help her, I want to get her to eat. 'What's your favourite food?' I say. 'Ham sandwiches,' she replies without hesitation. 'When's the last time you had a ham sandwich?' I ask. 'I can't remember,' she says sadly. 'Veronica,' I say, 'get a ham sandwich, cut it into four, look at it and think, "I'm going to have you". Try it Veronica. Please!'

And why don't I take my own advice? Because I don't care about myself; I don't give a toss what happens to me; I hate myself. But I care about Veronica: she's a nice person, she deserves to eat.

'You know,' I tell Veronica, 'people can die from this. So please go to the doctor, please get help. You can't do it on your own.' Veronica and I have warmed up a bit now. I take off my coat and Veronica unzips her jacket. I look at her tiny twig-like wrists and her scrawny neck poking out from her shirt, and I am stabbed through with jealousy. I can see that Veronica is ill, but I also see she's got a damn sight more control than me. Beside her, I feel like a prize heifer. 'But look at you,' says Veronica. 'You're thin and your skirt's too big for you.' 'Oh, it's a size too big,' I reply quickly.

It's Christmas Eve and I'm getting ready to go out for a drink with Kim. The doorbell goes. 'Gosh, Kim's early,' I think to myself as I finish off my make-up. I can hear her talking to Mum in the hall and thudding up the stairs. 'I'm nearly ready,' I call out. 'Claire,' says Kim seriously, as she comes into my room, 'I've got something to tell you.' 'What?' I ask, turning away from the mirror. 'It's Veronica,' she replies, starting to cry. 'She's dead isn't she?' I say, my own voice breaking. 'She went to the doctor's,' says Kim, trying to speak through her sobs, 'and they took her straight into hospital, but it was too late; she had a cardiac arrest.' I'm horrified; it's only been two weeks since Veronica and I talked in The Clarence. I can hardly take it in. Kim and I sit on my bed, clutching each other and crying our eyes out. 'It's such a shame,' says Kim, recovering a bit and blowing her nose. 'People don't realize what they're doing to themselves.' It doesn't cross my mind that she might be talking about me.

Chapter sixteen

Phew! It fits – my wedding dress fits. In fact it's too big; it'll have to be taken in. 'You want to be careful,' says the shop assistant through a mouthful of pins. 'I know it's natural for brides to lose a little weight before the wedding, but yours is nearly four months away – you don't want to lose any more.'

'If you get ill again we'll have to cancel the wedding,' says Mum. My weight is plummeting and Mum and Dad are worried sick. My new manager at Radio Rentals is concerned too. Jan's left and her replacement is Maureen Matthews, a little lady with blondish hair. I'm not sure how old she is – she'll never reveal her age or even her birthday. We are a small team at Radio Rentals – Maureen, me, and Andrea the part-timer.

I made Jan swear not to tell Maureen about my weekly appointments with Ruby. But I don't believe she's kept her promise because I trust no one – everyone is a potential enemy in the battle to make me fat. Maureen never questions me about where I go, so I'm convinced she knows.

'You know these appointments?' I say to Maureen one day when I'm cashing-up and she's watching the shop. 'Yes,' she says. 'Well,' I say, determined to find out whether Jan has betrayed me, 'it's because I had an eating problem.' And Maureen is genuinely surprised; she has no idea. She doesn't know anything about anorexia and wants to know more. I answer her questions. 'I'm alright now though,' I lie.

As the weeks roll by, Maureen and I become close. She's a wise, straight-talking, non-judgemental person and one day I admit to her what she already knows – that I still have a problem with food. She shows me nothing but sympathy and support.

Ruby is making noises about my going into hospital and Dr Pereira needing to see me. She's also trying to counsel me about the abuse. 'Let's talk about what happened, Claire,' she says. I feel a knot tighten in my stomach and shift uncomfortably in my seat. Talking about it is almost as bad as having to go through it. 'I can't,' I tell Ruby, getting upset. 'Why can't you?' she asks. 'I feel ashamed,' I mumble, tearfully. 'Why do you feel ashamed?' she insists. 'I just don't want to talk about it,' I say, crying openly. 'It's important that you talk about it,' Ruby counters. 'I can't,' I insist. 'It was my fault.' Time and time again Ruby will try to chip away at the subject, but she's always brought up short by the mental block I have about the abuse. 'It's my fault; I'm bad, bad, bad,' I say over and over, working myself into such a state that we simply can't continue.

As my weight drops I cancel my appointments with Ruby. I get away with it a few times. 'Hi Ruby,

I'm fine,' I say, 'but I can't make today's appointment; I've got a meeting,' or 'I've got to cover the shop because we're short-staffed.' But after a few weeks Ruby rings me. 'I need to see you, Claire,' she says. And when she does, oh dear!

My work skirt has fallen to my hip bones. Usually I wear as little as possible – if you're cold you burn more calories; but today I put on lots of layers so I'll weigh more when I step on Ruby's scales. I take off my shoes for the weigh-in, but keep on my jacket with a heavy bunch of keys and heaps of loose change in my pocket. Even so, the weight loss is dramatic. So much so that Ruby makes an appointment for me to see Dr Pereira. She wants Andy to come along too.

'Do you feel the need to womit?' asks Dr Pereira. I bite my lip and try not to laugh. I stare at the floor. I daren't look at Andy; if I do, I know we'll both get the giggles. 'Your weight is too low, Claire. I would like you to come into hospital, to get you better for your wedding,' says Dr Pereira, asking, 'How do you feel about that?' I don't want to be ill again, I want to be able to enjoy my wedding. Andy has been lobbying for me to go into hospital – he thinks I'm getting worse. So I agree to admit myself this afternoon. I go back to work and Maureen and Andrea are pleased and promise to visit me. I go home and it's a different story.

'If you go into the Faringdon Wing, I'm not visiting you,' shouts Dad. 'What have they ever done for you in there? You need to pull yourself to-bloody-gether and just eat.' Mum's not happy either. 'It didn't do you much good the last time,' says Mum, bitterly. 'When you came out you just started losing weight again.' 'I don't care what your parents say,' Andy tells me, 'I want you to go into hospital and get better.' I cling onto that: I'm hurt by my parents' reaction; they just don't understand.

———————————

I'm in Ward 18 this time, the post-acute admission ward, where there is more freedom. It's situated on two floors. The day area is on the ground floor and consists of a dining room, the main lounge where I played the piano during my last stay, and a smoking room leading onto the garden. There is also a crèche for the children of patients and staff. Upstairs are bedrooms and dormitories which are locked between 10 a.m. and noon, and 2 p.m. and 4 p.m., to stop patients lying in bed all day.

Dr Pereira has given me a new programme. Every day I have to eat breakfast, dinner and tea in the dining room. My main meal has to be meat, fish, eggs or cheese with salad and at least one piece of bread or one potato; plus a dessert – either fruit, cheese and biscuits, or ice cream. If I eat that for dinner then for tea I'm allowed just a sandwich but I still have to have another dessert. Three times a day, at 10 a.m., 3 p.m. and 8 p.m., I am supposed to have a cup of tea or coffee with milk and a snack – two biscuits, a piece of cake, or cheese and biscuits. I am to be weighed twice a week on a Tuesday and Friday before breakfast and am supposed to gain 2 pounds per week to reach my target weight of 8 stone 6. They put my current weight at 7 stone 7. The programme also says that I must approach staff after meals if I feel the need to be sick, and, where possible, I have to keep staff posted as to my whereabouts for two hours following meals.

If I do not comply with the programme then my privileges will start to be revoked. Sarah, my new keyworker, gives me some examples – if I miss my snacks then my telephone calls will be limited. If I miss dinner or tea then my visitors will be limited. If I leave the ward without informing anyone my listening to music will be limited. For 'limited' read 'stopped'. Also, if I do not gain a pound on each weighing day, then I must remain on the ward until the next weighing day. If, however, I meet my weight targets I am allowed to go out with friends and my fiancé.

Being on Ward 18 is a bad move because patients have more freedom than on Ward 17. I sit on my own in the dining room and siphon food into my handbag. Most of the nurses don't seem to have a clue about the conditions in my programme so I tell them I'm allowed out and they take my word for it. I've been waltzing over the road to the chemist, and writing out whacking great cheques for dozens of tablets. I am swallowing laxatives, slimming tablets which expand in your stomach so you don't want to eat and diuretics which are supposed to be used to combat water retention. The urge to take them is just too strong for me to resist.

Andy comes up every night. Mum, who works at the hospital, visits a couple of times a day – I knew she couldn't stay away. My friend Simone comes up from London. I'm sitting in my room with my brother Michael and Maureen from work, when she walks in. She's bearing a huge box of 'Roses' chocolates. Michael and Maureen look at her as if she's mad, but I understand why she's brought them. That's what you do when people are ill – buy them chocolates. It was her way of saying, 'You're ill and I wish you better'. I am grateful to her for the normality of the gesture and eat one.

After a week, Dad relents and comes to visit. He and Mum sit with me in the lounge, tightlipped. They can see I'm no better. I don't know it, but later Dad has a go at one of the nurses. 'She's getting worse,' he starts. 'What exactly are you doing for her? She's treating this place like a bloody holiday camp. People have seen her out shopping – can't you stop her? She'll be buying laxatives!' 'She's not a compulsory patient,' explains the nurse. 'Well make her compulsory. Section her for God's sake!' he retorts, slamming out of the building.

────────────

'Hello, are you Claire?' I am sitting in reception talking to my friend Kim Speight who's come to see me. 'Yes,' I say, glancing up to see an intense-looking woman with long hair. Snooty cow – she's looking down her nose at me and her eyes are darting about, sizing me up. 'My name's Lorna Franklin. Dr Pereira has asked me to have a word with you,' she says. 'I run a self-help group for people with similar problems to your own and I'd like to chat to you about it,' she finishes. 'What, now?' I say, defensively. 'Yes,' she says, glancing over at Kim. 'Alright,' I say, thinking, 'What can *she* possibly know about my problem?'

Lorna takes me into one of the occupational therapy rooms and tells me about the group which she started recently. 'The main aim is to get people together so they can share how they feel. Often people think it is only happening to them, and they find it helpful to talk about their problems with others who understand. The group lasts for an hour and a half and we have a break half-way through,' explains Lorna, who is a psychiatric nurse. She continues, 'In the first half I go round the group asking each person how their week has been and focusing on particular difficulties they might be having; but there is no pressure on you to say anything if you don't want to. In the second half we might talk about body image, the links between stress and eating disorders, or look at healthy eating and lifestyles.' Part of me feels quite inquisitive, part of me feels threatened – there are bound to be lots of girls there who are thinner than me.

'I know you are being treated for anorexia. How long have you had a problem with food?' Lorna asks. I flinch at the word 'anorexia', but I tell her. I also talk about my friend Veronica, so Lorna will know I'm not that ill. 'Veronica really did have anorexia; I mean, she died,' I say, adding, 'but I'm not like that.' 'Why aren't you like that?' asks Lorna. 'Because those people are thin,' I say, 'and I'm not, am I?' 'You look emaciated,' says Lorna and, perversely, I feel pleased. Looking at her watch, Lorna says, 'If you stay in reception, I'll come and get you in 20 minutes and take you along to the group.'

I wander back to reception where Kim is waiting. 'What did she say, Claire?' she asks, and I tell her. Kim takes hold of my hands. 'Look at your hands,' she says, her voice breaking. 'They're so tiny. Go to the group; please.'

At half-past seven Lorna arrives to collect me. I say my goodbyes to Kim and follow Lorna to the room where we talked earlier. Lorna opens the door and introduces me to the group of people who are sitting in a circle. There's another nurse called Mike and three girls. The only one I'm interested in is Wendy. I can't see her face, just her cap of blonde hair, and black leggings which hang loosely about her legs. I can't keep my eyes off her – she is so *thin*. Lorna shows me to an empty chair and I sit, my eyes glued to the little girl opposite.

Lorna's going round the room asking people how they've been feeling over the last week. It seems the other two girls are bulimic. 'I'm fed up with spending half my life down the toilet,' one of them says. 'How disgusting,' I think. Then Lorna starts on at Wendy. Sitting there with her head bowed, shrouded in a huge black jumper, she reminds me so much of Veronica. 'I don't really want to say anything,' whispers Wendy. Lorna asks her a few questions and she answers simply yes or no. I listen intently. I'm aghast. It seems that Wendy isn't even in hospital; she's still working. I can't believe it. Here I am in hospital and she's much thinner than me! I glare at Wendy.

'Do you want to say anything, Claire?' says Lorna. 'Not really,' I say shortly. 'Have you got a problem?' Lorna persists. 'Yeah,' I say angrily, staring at Wendy, 'I've got a problem – I'm too big!' I catch a look between Lorna and Mike. I bet they think I binge. 'I don't binge though,' I say quickly. 'I never binge.'

'Right, we'll have a break now,' says Lorna. 'Is there somewhere I can go for a cigarette?' I ask.

'Yes,' says Lorna, 'you can go outside into reception.' I walk into reception and there she is, there's Wendy. I can't keep my eyes off her. I sit in the spare seat next to her so I can study her more closely. I am puffing furiously on my fag and scrutinizing her out of the corner of my eye. I can see she's doing the same. 'Oh, Claire,' I think to myself, 'just say something to the girl.' 'Do you like The Carpenters?' I ask her. 'Yeah,' says Wendy, turning her little face towards me. 'Yeah, I do.' 'Put it there,' I say, holding out my hand and she lets me shake her scrawny hand.

'How long have you been coming to the group?' I ask. 'A few weeks,' she replies. 'Do you like it?' I ask. 'Not really,' she says. 'I've got to come; the doctor makes me come.' As we talk, I recognize a kindred spirit. 'Do you feel like you're really big, and that every time you eat something – no matter how small it is – you feel like you've put on a stone?' I ask her. 'Yes,' she replies. 'I feel like that too,' I say. 'But you're so skinny!' she exclaims. 'How can you say that?' I reply, 'I'm massive compared to you.' 'But you're not,' she says. 'Look at you in those green cords – your hip bones are almost piercing the fabric. And your arms in that little cream jumper, they're like sticks.' The envy in her voice is obvious, and I suddenly realize that she feels as threatened by me as I do by her.

Wendy and I become friendly. She comes to visit me after she's finished work. 'Let's go up to Junction 11 and have a coffee,' she suggests one day. 'Okay,' I say and we go up to Junction 11, the main hospital cafeteria, where all the doctors and nurses go. We hunch over our Diet Cokes in the smoking section and chat. 'Did any of you see that programme on anorexia the other night?' says a voice, loud and obvious, from the table next to ours. I look over and see a group of nurses eyeing us. I turn back and concentrate on my Coke. 'I can't understand it,' the voice continues. 'All they need is a good meal.' The rest of the table break into titters. I look at Wendy and she looks at me. 'I don't feel comfortable here,' I say. 'Nor do I,' she replies, 'let's go.' We post our cigarette butts into our Coke cans, shove back our chairs and leave.

I manipulate Wendy. The nurses have got wise to my lies and I'm only allowed off the ward with a member of staff. It's impossible for me to buy laxatives. 'Wendy, please. You've got to help me,' I say, feeding money into the pay phone. 'You've got to bring me 60 Senokot this evening.' 'But Claire, I'm not allowed to,' says Wendy, her voice uncertain. 'You know how you'd feel if you couldn't get laxatives,' I wheedle. My friend's umming and ahhing on the other end of the phone. I step up the pressure. 'Wendy, listen to me,' I say. 'If you don't get me some Senokot, I'll probably kill myself, because I can't hack it any longer.' Poor Wendy; under duress, she agrees to bring me some tablets. 'I'm not very happy about this,' she says later, handing over the Senokot. 'Thank you,' I reply. 'You've saved my life.'

———

It's Saturday and I've got a special dispensation to go into town with my cousin Jannine to show her my wedding dress. Not the actual one, because it's still being altered, but the sample they keep in the shop. I'm so weak I'm unsteady on my feet and have trouble pushing the dresses along the rail. Out of the corner of my eye I see the assistants gasping in horror at me. I'm not surprised, I look a state: I've no make-up on and my hair's a mess. 'Here it is, here's my dress,' I say, trying to lift the frock off the rail. It's so heavy, Jannine has to help me.

Later Jannine drags me into Next. She insists that I try on some clothes. I pick out a red dress in size 14. 'You're not size 14!' exclaims Jannine. 'Try the 8!' She's trying to prove a point to me. 'There, look,' she says, pulling at the skirt. 'Can't you see it's miles too big and it's only a size 8?' 'Yeah,' I reply, 'but the size 8s in Next are very generous.'

I do have flashes of reality when I know that I'm very ill and in danger of going into cardiac or renal failure, of getting osteoporosis in years to come – the doctors have told me often enough. Then I know that I need food to live a normal life; that it is only when I eat that my periods will come back and I'll be able to have children with Andy. And I try, I really try to eat but when I do the demonic voice in my head comes back, and it's so powerful. 'You're bad, you're fat,' it rings in my ears, making me feel guilty and bloated. It throws me into a panic, and I guzzle down laxatives or make myself sick to get rid of the feelings, to get rid of the voice. Then I feel guilty all over again: I'll go and tell a nurse that I've got laxatives, hand them over, then immediately regret it. Sometimes I think the conflict inside my head will make it split.

'How are you?' says Lorna when I bump into her in reception one day. 'I've gained a pound,' I reply, tearfully. 'A pound's nothing,' says Lorna reassuringly, 'and you are very emaciated.' 'But I'm not! I'm not!' I insist, adding, 'look, let me show you my stomach.' I drag Lorna into the Ladies, lift up my top and show her my stomach. 'Look! Look at it!' I say, starting to cry at the sight of my disgusting body in the mirror. 'Claire,' says Lorna gently, 'all I can see is bone. And look at your pelvic bones,' she says, touching them, 'they're going to come through your skin soon.' 'But I feel so awful,' I wail, wringing my hands. 'I know,' says Lorna softly, giving me a hug, 'I know.' She holds me until I can't cry any more; and a bond begins to form between us.

'It doesn't matter what they say,' I tell Andy, 'we're getting married and that's that.' Dr Pereira has been trying to persuade Andy and me to postpone the wedding. But I'm having none of it. We're sitting in my room doing our wedding list. We're flicking through the Argos catalogue choosing things and chatting about the future. 'I'm really going to get better, Andy,' I say. 'I've been thinking,' says Andy. 'You know how much you love The Carpenters? Well, why don't we have "We've Only Just Begun" for the first dance?' 'Really?' I say, 'I really can?' 'You really can,' he says, laughing and giving me a little kiss. Chattering happily we decide on a lawnmower, a cookie jar, some towels. 'We'll need some scales,' I say casually. Andy stares at me in disbelief. 'Well,' I say, 'I'm going to get better, and everybody's got to have scales in their bathroom, haven't they?' Andy agrees; and do you know, I am so convincing, I almost convince myself. 'You know,' I say, pushing my luck a little further, 'if people give us enough Argos vouchers we could get an exercise bike for your gym.'

Chapter seventeen

I can't wait to get out of here. I'm sick of the regimented meal-times, the boredom, the endless cigarettes. I'm smoking between 40 and 60 cigarettes a day: it gives me something to do and stifles the hunger pangs. I have a constant dry throat, my clothes and hair stink of smoke and my fingers are yellow with nicotine. I feel lethargic all the time; I can't even be bothered to read and play the piano any more. Thinking of ways of getting to the chemist so I can buy more laxatives is the only thing I have any enthusiasm for.

I've been going on and on to Dr Pereira. 'I'm going. I'm discharging myself,' I keep saying. He persuades me to stay for one more week. He reduces my target weight to 8 stone 2 – I told him 8 stone 6 was totally unrealistic – and he says he'd like me to be at least 7 stone 11 by the time I leave hospital next week. At home I'm to follow a maintenance diet drawn up by a dietician to increase my weight to 8 stone 2.

'Good luck with your wedding,' says Dr Pereira.

It's Tuesday, 9th March. I've filled myself to the brim with Diet Coke and got the scales to say 7 stone 13. Dr Pereira is discharging me reluctantly, under a battery of promises to come back and see him, to carry on seeing Ruby at Beacon House, and to continue going to Lorna's group. He hands me the maintenance diet which goes straight in the bin. Yippee! I'm free.

There's a little over a month to go before our wedding on 17th April. I'm back at work and busy organizing things for the big day. I have a final fitting for the wedding dress – it fits, thank God. I choose head-dresses for me and my sister Lisa and Kim Speight, who are going to be bridesmaids.

'Can I have something different?' I ask when the caterers come to Mum and Dad's to discuss the menu. We've settled on chicken in a sauce, but I prefer simple things. 'Can I have bangers and mash?' I say, and everybody laughs. 'You're the bride,' says Mum, smiling with pleasure, 'you can have what you want!'

Two Fridays before the wedding day, Andy and I spend the night in our house as usual. We've bought a brand-new king-size bed and, although we don't plan to, we make love for the first time. It's nothing to write home about, but I feel relieved to have got it out of the way. Now worrying about the wedding night isn't going to ruin my big day.

Saturday is the hen and stag night. Andy's going bowling with his mates and he's really worried they're going to strip him and leave him somewhere. He's thinking of not going! I'm spending the evening with a big gang of girlfriends; Mum and Lisa are coming too. I go into town and splash out

30 quid on a black lacy top with flarey sleeves from Snob which I'm wearing with a pair of black trousers. The top shows your midriff and I have to wear a black bra underneath it. It's really daring for me, but my stomach is flat and my pelvic bones stick out, and I can see the bones running horizontally across my chest. I run my fingers over them: I feel okay; I feel slim.

We meet in The Sugar Loaf pub and go on to The Ritzy nightclub. Claire McCann has made me a dress out of a black binliner and pinned lots of rude weddingy things all over it – condoms, paper horseshoes, pictures of nude men and headlines she's cut out from tabloid newspapers saying things like 'Women on Top'. She's also fastened a bit of white net to a white floppy straw hat and pinned Radio Rentals badges all over it. I put on the binliner and the hat and make an effort to chat and laugh. I don't drink much; in fact, it comes to 12 o'clock and I want to go home. 'You can't go home,' says Mum, 'all your friends are here!' So I have a dance with my mates and go up to each of the three bars and say 'It's my hen night,' and get three free bottles of champagne. To Mum's amazement, this bloke comes up and asks her to dance: 'No thank you,' she says primly, and when he turns away we all laugh.

Flap, flap, flap; the wedding's not till three this afternoon but everybody's in a terrible flap. The band have rung – they don't think there's enough power in the church hall for all their equipment. Panic! We're all worrying about the best man. He didn't show for the rehearsal at the church yesterday –

Andy found him fishing on the canal! Will he show at all today – and if he does, will he remember the rings? I'm a bundle of nerves and don't feel like eating, but I stuff down a couple of pieces of toast to keep Mum happy.

Lisa's putting rollers in my hair when the doorbell rings. Mum comes running upstairs with a single red rose in a clear plastic box. 'See you at three; love – your husband-to-be,' reads the card. I am choked with happiness.

The bouquets arrive. The flowers are all peaches and creams and tied with green satin ribbons to match the bridesmaids' dresses. Kim comes over and the hairdresser arrives. She puts up my hair and arranges the silk flower head-dress. I put on my make-up and race around, my wedding face and hair sitting incongruously above my jeans and T-shirt until it's time to put on the dress.

I'm changing in the bedroom I used to share with Lisa because there's more space. I slip into the lacy off-white basque which matches the dress. I catch a look passing between Kim and Lisa as my chest bones are briefly on display. I pull on a pair of white 'hold-up' stockings, except they don't because my legs are so thin, so I have to wear a suspender belt as well. 'Something borrowed' is a pearl necklace and earrings belonging to Andrea, whom I work with. I class my engagement ring as 'something old'; the dress is 'something new' and my blue garter is 'something blue'. 'Oh, you look absolutely stunning,' says Mum, a proud wet smile on her face.

Then it's all systems go. Dad's brushing dog hair off his tails and Mum's patting into place the peach hat which matches her outfit. The photographer arrives, Auntie Pat and Uncle Sid turn up and Uncle Sid starts fiddling about with his video recorder. 'Don't forget to take the lens cap off!' laughs Dad. The vintage Austin draws up, and out steps the driver with his grey peaked cap, jacket and breeches.

The house is emptying as Mum and the brides-maids go up to the church. 'It's just you and me sweetheart,' says Dad as he takes my arm. 'Don't Dad, you'll make me cry,' I say, shivering a little in my big dress. It's a fine day, but quite cold. A straggle of neighbours are out on the pavement watching our progress down the drive. 'Doesn't she look lovely!' they say. 'Good luck!' they call. 'This is it,' I think to myself as the photographer flashes away.

Dad's paid a lot of money for the car, so instead of driving straight to the church we drive past The Favourite pub, on past the church and the hall where the reception's going to be, past my old school, Lealands High. We go as far as Sundon Park, round the roundabout and then come back. We pass Grand-ma and Granddad's house, but it doesn't cross my mind to look.

When we pull up at the church, the bridesmaids and the photographer are waiting on the concrete forecourt. The photographer wants to take a picture of Dad helping me out of the little maroon car. So we do it in slow motion and pose. Lisa has to keep running in because she's cold, but Kim helps arrange my train for the photographer. Dad and I walk to the door of the church and a few stragglers nip in ahead of us. A whisper of 'she's here, she's here,' whips through the pews. Putting our best feet forward Dad and I march through the door. I don't hear the music or see the congregation. 'Did they actually play "Here Comes the Bride"?' I'll ask later.

'Wow!' mouths Andy as I draw level with him. Father Denis says a few words and then together we walk up the steps to the altar where Andy and I each light a candle. My hands are shaking and Andy takes my arm and guides it to the candle. Then we kneel down and make our vows. Richard, thank God, has remembered the rings.

———————

Down the aisle we go, dizzy with happiness. The bells start and so does the rain. We walk out of the church door, and with dismay I notice drops marking my dress. 'Happy is the bride the sun shines on; happy is the corpse the rain falls on.' Isn't that what they say?

He's a little Hitler, the photographer. For what seems like hours he makes us line and realign for photos. First it's the bride's family, then the groom's, then the ushers, then us getting into the car. Oops – nearly forgot, the friends' photograph! Mum is worrying that the meal is drying up next door and the crowd is getting restless. At least one friend – Claire McCann – has gone to the pub! 'Smile, smile,' orders the photographer. My mouth is split in a permanent inane grin and I hardly notice Grandma slipping a silver plastic horseshoe on a white ribbon over my wrist.

'Can I have some more please?' I say to one of the waitresses. Dad and Andy, who are sitting next to me on the top table, exchange glances. 'Yes,' I say, laughing, 'I have turned over a new leaf!' And I truly, truly mean it. After speeches and toasts everybody helps push back the tables ready for the band and the disco. Mum and Dad are breathing a sigh of relief to see that the band have got round the power problem and are beginning to tune-up.

The band really get the party going. Mum and Dad first saw them at Caesar's Palace in Milton Keynes and paid £800 for them to play for an hour, but they are really worth it. They're called The Itsy Bitsy Showband and they sing and do comedy impressions. 'Here's an impression of Roy Orbison,' says the lead singer. Then he lies down on the floor with his arms crossed on his chest. Everybody falls about! Then they start picking on Jan, my ex-manager at Radio Rentals; going on about her big boobs. She loves it and we are all in stitches.

Then the disco kicks off with the first dance 'We've Only Just Begun'. The lights dim; Andy guides me to the centre of the dance floor and puts his arms around me. One by one, people flick on their cigarette lighters and all we can see in the darkness is a blur of waving light. I feel like I've died and gone to heaven.

———————

'You look too young to be getting married,' comments the lady cab driver who's driving us away from the reception to our new home. 'How old are you?' 'Twenty-two,' I reply. 'I thought you were only about sixteen or seventeen,' she says.

Getting out of the taxi, Andy and I attract a lot of attention from people walking home from the pub. I'm still in my bride dress, Andy's in his tails: he picks me up and carries me over the threshold, and the knot of people standing on the pavement cheer. Laughing, he deposits me on the settee where I kick off my heels and sprawl. I shake confetti from my dress and out of my hair: it's all over the carpet. Andy comes through from the kitchen with two mugs of tea and I reach for a cigarette. I haven't had one since before the wedding – I didn't think it'd look nice, smoking in my beautiful dress. We talk about the brilliant day we've had; and then go to bed, exhausted.

Bless them, Catherina and Daffy have come over to cook us breakfast. 'It was the best wedding we've ever been to,' they say, piling through the front door with fresh bread, rashers and eggs. 'Are you better?' asks Catherina quietly as we cook breakfast. 'Yes,' I say, 'don't I look better?' 'Nope,' she says, 'you're legs are like matchsticks.'

I feel better though. I'm off on our honeymoon and I very deliberately left laxatives off my list of things to pack. As I say, I'm turning over a new leaf. We are flying out to Marbella where we are going to stay in Andy's Mum's time-share. 'You'll never guess who's behind us?' whispers Andy as we stand in line at the airport. 'Who?' I say, whizzing round. It's the black girl who plays Gerry in my favourite television soap *Eldorado*. You know, the one who always wears dungarees and hangs around with the gay bloke Freddy. She looks exactly the same as she does on telly. 'Are you who I think you are?' I ask her. 'That depends who you think I am,' she replies, laughing. 'I love your programme,' I say. 'I'm gutted that it's going to be axed.' We chat for a few minutes. She's on her way out to the *Eldorado* set. 'This is making your honeymoon, isn't it!' says Andy, as 'Gerry' wanders off to get herself a Coke. 'Yes,' I agree, laughing, 'and if I could get a T-shirt saying "I love Eldorado" I would!'

With marble floors, a balcony, a swimming pool and views over the mountains, the apartment is perfect. It's very hot and by the time we go out for a meal on our first night, I've got a little red nose and burnt cheeks. I am so happy. I am eating pretty much what I like. 'Stuff it, I'm on holiday,' I say to myself. But the meals do tend to be greasy and usually come with chips, and during the week I occasionally feel a bit panicky. But all in all we are having a great time. Andy and I don't talk about my illness; we just concentrate on enjoying ourselves.

We're having sex all the time. He'll be putting suntan lotion on my back. I'll look at him, he'll look at me and we'll have to go indoors. It's four o'clock in the afternoon when 'ding dong' the doorbell goes. 'Avon calling,' I laugh. 'It's your mum,' Andy says. 'It's your mum,' I reply. 'Hang on, we're married!' we both say and laugh. 'They'll go away,' says Andy; but next minute a key rattles in the lock, the door opens and a Spanish workman's watching us making love. I dive under the covers in embarrassment and Andy grabs a towel and stammers, 'Er, we're a bit busy now.' The guy looks horrified. 'Oh! oh!' he cries before turning on his heel and racing out of the door.

Our balcony looks over a riding stables. 'I'll take you riding,' I say to Andy, and book us a two-hour session. Although I haven't had any lessons, I have ridden before and know what to do. Andy has never been on a horse, but I assume that somebody will make sure he's alright. Wrong. I've inadvertently booked into a session for experienced riders, and to make matters worse, Andy, being tall, is given a huge stallion. Up into the mountains we climb. 'You can gallop if you like,' calls the guy in charge. I go for it. 'Divorce!' shouts Andy as his horse takes its lead from mine and starts cantering. I turn round to see him clinging to his horse's mane, his saddle twisting to one side underneath him. The instructor halts the party and, as we stop, thankfully so does Andy's horse. I can't help laughing. 'I was so scared,' says Andy, 'I was plaiting my hair into his mane for extra grip!'

A week later, the honeymoon's over. It's Sunday afternoon, and we're all at Mum and Dad's – Lisa, Michael and his girlfriend Elaine, Kim and her boyfriend Ronnie. Andy and I are opening our wedding presents and everyone's watching and exclaiming. There's a king-size quilt set and some money from Grandma, and a clock from Andy's work colleagues. I pick up a square-shaped present and begin to tear off the paper. It's a set of electronic scales. I see Kim giving Ronnie a sideways look, and quickly put the scales down and go on to the next package. Later Andy and I drive home, the huge pile of gifts filling the back of the car. Somewhere in there lie the scales – an unexploded bomb waiting to go off.

We carry all the presents into our front room and Andy goes into the kitchen to make a cup of tea.

Quick as a flash, I pick up the scales and set them in the middle of the floor. Soundlessly I step onto them. The red illuminated numbers flicker and settle: 8 stone 7! 'I can't cope with this,' I think to myself in horror. 'I can't cope with being this big!'

Chapter eighteen

I am cutting down. I miss breakfast and dinner and just have my tea in the evening. I'll do Andy a baked potato, salad and chicken Kiev, but I'll only have a baked potato and salad. By the end of the first week I've lost half a stone. I feel lighter, more comfortable, happier with myself – confident even. 'I'll just lose another half a stone,' I think to myself.

Several weeks later I am on my way to do the banking for Radio Rentals. I am passing Boots. 'I want to buy some laxatives,' I think. 'No, Claire,' I say to myself, 'you don't want to get into that again.' I'm trying to pay off a £700 overdraft which I ran up buying tablets before. But I can't stop myself. Deep down I know what I'm doing is wrong but the urge to lose weight is too strong. It sounds crazy, but starving and abusing laxatives is less stressful than eating and being big. I go in and buy 60 Dulcolax. I take 10 that night and feel dreadful the next day. Ten Dulcolax seem to have the same effect on me as 40 or 50 Senokot. Trouble is, my body hardens to them. I up the amount to 20 Dulcolax a day, then 30, 40, 50, then 60 a day. It's costing me a fortune, but I can't stop myself.

I'm sick of Diet Coke so I go into Boots to check out their 'Shapers' range. Ah, 'Cloudy Lemonade' – one calorie per can. I start to allow myself a can a day. I also drink tea and coffee – with two sweeteners and no milk. 'Oh, look at your arms, they're blue and you're so cold to the touch,' says Andrea at work.

'I've bought you a Kit Kat,' says Maureen. 'I don't want it,' I say. 'Just have half – just have two fingers.' 'No, I can't,' I say. 'Just have one finger,' chivvies Maureen. 'Go on.' 'Okay, I'll have one finger,' I say. I *want* the Kit Kat. I am starving, literally. Hunger eats at me day and night. Maureen's giving me permission to let something pass my lips; she's saying I deserve it. I'm finding it difficult to buy anything for myself now – not just food, but clothes, records, even a magazine. I don't feel I deserve anything nice. The only things I buy are laxatives and fags – but that's okay, they're bad for you.

Slowly I open the Kit Kat and break off one finger. I nibble round the edge of the finger and gnaw off the chocolate which covers it. Only then do I eat the wafer. Maureen also buys me iced buns – she knows I like them. Once she catches me shoving bits of bun up my sleeve. 'Claire,' she says firmly, 'don't insult my intelligence. The only person you are hurting is yourself.' But I don't care about myself. I hate upsetting other people though, Maureen, Andy, my mum and dad. In a way I wish they didn't care because I can't bear to see them worrying. I start pretending I'm okay, pretending to be normal.

'I'm fine,' I say, acting happy and bubbly. 'I cooked Andy and me this lovely pasta dish last night,' I tell Maureen and Andrea, willing them to believe that I'd eaten it. I bake for Andy – ginger cake, scones, rock buns – and take some in for the girls. 'I won't have one. I don't want to see another rock bun. I stuffed myself with them last night,' I fib. I work harder than ever. If there's hoovering to be done, 'I'll do it,' I say. If there is a new display to arrange, 'Let me, you put your feet up.' If there is banking to be done, 'Don't worry, I'll go.' I have to prove I'm okay, to stop them going on at me; and of course the more I do, the more calories I burn off.

It's hard work trying to be normal. I keep the charade up at the shop, but as soon as I get home my mask slips. I'm tired and low and if I've had anything extra to eat I feel huge and really down in the dumps. 'Do I look big?', 'Do I look bigger than when we got married?', 'Do I look bigger than when we first met?' On and on I go about my weight. 'No you don't look big,' says Andy gently, adding, 'you could do with putting on some weight.' But I don't believe him; I think he's just saying it.

'Get it sorted this time,' says Andy, dropping me off at the Faringdon Wing for Lorna's group. We're rowing and our love-life has fizzled out. I can hardly walk, let alone have sex. I have on a size 8 pair of jeans and they have fallen to my hips, and they are not supposed to be hipsters. The hair on my head is dry, dull and falling out; and a coat of downy fur is creeping over my belly and up my spine – my body's attempt at keeping itself warm. No amount of make-up can disguise my pale spotty skin or the dark shadows under my eyes. I can't shave my underarm hair any more as the flesh has shrunk into the hollows of my bones.

I am so starved that once every two weeks I end up having a massive binge, usually on my day-off. I eat the entire middle tier of my wedding cake, the one Andy and I were saving for the christening of our first child. One minute I'm tasting a crumb of icing on the tip of my tongue, the next the cake tin's empty and I'm crawling on the floor groaning, a beached whale. On Sundays I go to dance aerobics – it takes every ounce of energy and determination to do the class, and by the time I get back I am shaky with fatigue. Andy's usually at his Mum's for Sunday dinner, so while he's away I dive into the biscuit barrel. My body's craving sugar but I don't allow myself to eat the biscuits. I put them in my mouth and chew them, savouring the sugary taste. Then instead of swallowing, I spit the soggy mess into a wodge of kitchen towel and throw it away.

'Claire, you look so ill,' says Lorna quietly. I am the only person attending the group today. 'I'm fine,' I respond robotically. 'You don't look fine,' she replies, adding, 'The only reason you're saying you're fine is because admitting you have a problem means you're going to have to do something about it.' 'I'm fine,' I insist. 'How much do you weigh?' asks Lorna. 'Seven and a half, eight stone,' I reply. 'You are well below that and you know it. I'd say you are six and a half, if that,' she says. 'Please let me weigh you.' I struggle to get out of the chair, intending to leg it. 'It's okay, Claire,' sighs Lorna. 'Sit down. I won't weigh you.' She looks at me for a minute and says, 'How far would you take your clothes off so I could take a photo of you?' 'You are not getting a camera near me,' I say, adamant. I am too fat, too repulsive to photograph. Anyway photographs prove that I exist – I want to disappear.

'You're not keeping your appointments with Ruby, and everybody's concerned about you, Claire,' continues Lorna. 'There's nothing wrong with me. Why can't you lot just leave me alone?' I retort. 'The doctors are going to have no alternative but to section you under the Mental Health Act,' says Lorna, 'and that's not a threat. They *will* come and get you, kicking and screaming.' 'I'm fine,' I insist. I'm terrified of being sectioned. My life will be in enemy hands – even my family won't have a say in what happens to me. I'll be forced into hospital against my will, forced to stay for six months, forced to have treatment, force-fed to be fat. 'Claire, if we didn't care, we wouldn't be persevering,' says Lorna, softly. 'Well, don't care,' I snap. 'I'm not asking you to care.'

'Look at the state of you,' says Lisa. 'You need help,' says Michael. 'You're just emaciated,' says Andy. 'For God's sake, Claire! We can't handle it any more,' pleads Mum. Mum, Michael and Lisa are sitting in a row on the settee; Andy's perched on the arm. I am curled up in the armchair opposite, staring at them blankly. 'There's nothing wrong with me,' I reply in a low voice. Inside I'm screaming, 'Fuck off and leave me alone!' 'You look disgusting,' says Michael. That's it, I'm not listening to this. 'Please go into hospital,' begs Mum. I explode, 'You didn't want me to go in there in February and you were right, weren't you? It didn't do me any good. So I'm not going in there now!' I slam out of the room.

I am standing on the electronic weighing scales in Boots. I've been really cutting down. I've been having a can of 'Cloudy Lemonade' for dinner and a slice of cheese for tea. I look down at the scales. They say 5 stone 10. 'I remember when I had a lovely slim figure like yours,' smiles a passer-by. That's it, that just takes the biscuit. I am being told I'm going to be sectioned and there's nothing wrong with me. This woman's proved it – she doesn't know me and she thinks I've got a lovely figure!

'You liar!' I fly at Lorna, when I see her at the group that night. 'Calm down, Claire,' she says. 'Calm down and tell me what's happened.' 'How could you do that to me?' I yell. 'What?' asks Lorna, watching me pace up and down the room. I gabble out the story of the woman in Boots. 'If the woman had looked at you closely, she would have seen that you are extremely ill,' replies Lorna, gently. I pick up a heavy paperweight made of rock from the table, and toss it between my hands as I listen to her babble. 'Are you going to throw that at my head?' she says, looking alarmed. 'No,' I say, with the hint of a smile, and put the paperweight down.

I'm not going to hurt Lorna: I feel that she's the first person who can see beyond my body to the sad person underneath. She listens when I need to talk, she advises when I need advice, she hugs me when I need to be held, and passes the tissues when I need to cry. She spends hours with me. 'I know you find food frightening,' she says, 'but you deserve food, and your body needs nourishment.' She never gives up. When everyone else is letting me get away with blue murder she challenges me. 'I know you're cheating the scales, Claire,' she'll say matter-of-factly. 'The only person you're hurting is yourself.' And when I retort, 'I don't care!' she replies, 'Well I do.'

She works and works at building up my self-esteem, trying to get me to focus on what she perceives as my good points, where I can't see any.

'Now you either come up to the hospital by three o'-clock or we're coming to get you,' says Ruby on the other end of the phone. 'I'm busy in the shop,' I retort. 'You are not busy,' insists Ruby. 'I've spoken to your boss and she's allowing you to come and see us.' 'How dare you!' I scream in rage. 'How dare you speak to Maureen about me.' 'Claire,' continues Ruby, 'it is imperative that we see you. Now you either get up to the hospital by three o'clock or we'll come to get you. It's your choice.' I slam down the phone. 'I'm going out,' I say, glaring at Maureen.

'Wendy!' I think, walking out of the shop, 'she'll help me.' I start running to the building where Wendy works. I fling open the double doors and race down the corridor, banging on every door. 'Wendy!' I'm shouting, 'Wendy!' 'Calm down,' says a woman, coming out of one of the offices, 'we'll find her.' Wendy comes rushing out of her office, and guides me out of the building.

'Claire,' she says, 'what's the matter?' 'You've got to hide me Wendy! They're coming to take me away,' I gabble. 'Sit down,' says Wendy, pointing to a bench. 'Now, have a fag.' She sits me down and lights my cigarette. 'Claire,' she says, 'you look awful. Look at your clothes; they're hanging off you. You're skin and bone. You're really ill and I think you're going to die. Please go into hospital. Don't let them come and get you, you won't be able to handle it.' 'No,' I say desperately, 'I'll run away.'

'Claire,' replies Wendy, 'you can't, they'll send the police to find you.'

I go – not to hospital, but home. I sit on the stairs and smoke cigarette after cigarette. All sorts of thoughts go through my head – of running away, of going to Ireland. But I'm up to my ears in debt and haven't got enough money. 'Ding, dong!' I freeze. They've come for me. I can see a shadow at the door. 'Ding, dong!' I can hear my heart pounding, it's so loud. Surely they can hear it too. 'Knock knock knock', they're rapping on the door now. 'Please go away, please go away,' I'm thinking. And they do: I hear footsteps turn away and walk up the hill. I creep to the door of the front room and I can see her through the window, a lady with a briefcase getting into a car marked 'Doctor' parked on the double yellow lines outside.

I dart upstairs and start packing. I don't know what I'm packing for; I don't know what I'm doing. Then I hear Andy's key in the lock and the phone going at the same time. He walks in and picks up the phone and I can hear him saying, 'Let me talk to her.' It's obviously Ruby. Slowly I come downstairs gesturing and mouthing to Andy, 'Please don't make me go now; I'll go Friday.' 'Can Claire come in the day after tomorrow, Ruby?' says Andy into the mouthpiece. 'Okay,' says Ruby, and I breathe a sigh of relief.

———————

It's Friday – I've hidden some laxatives under the lining of my holdall and packed my stuff on top. Ruby collects me and drives to the Faringdon Wing where she takes me to one of the interview rooms off Ward 17. 'Wait here, Claire,' she says. 'I'm just going to pop down and get your notes.' 'One two, three...' I count to ten, grab my bag and run for it. As I charge through the double-doors out onto the landing I hear a shout: 'Stop her!' I look back over my shoulder and a second later two male nurses have hold of me. 'Get off me!' I yell, dropping my bag and flailing with my arms.

I'm back in the interview room with Ruby and the nurse Editha. 'Hello, Claire,' says Dr Pinto walking in. 'Hello,' I hiss viciously. 'I don't think you should leave at present,' he says. 'You can't bloody keep me here,' I spit. 'There's nothing wrong with me. Now let me go.' 'Will you or will you not stay in hospital under your own steam?' Dr Pinto asks. 'No!' I reply quickly, 'I'm doing better now. You are wasting your time, wasting everybody's time. There is nothing wrong with me. I am eating and I'm putting on weight.' 'What is your weight now, Claire?' asks Dr Pinto. 'Seven and a half stone,' I say defiantly. 'Okay, Editha, could you weigh Claire please? I'll be back in a minute.' I step onto the scales with some degree of confidence – I did the drink trick this morning, so I should be alright. Sure enough, 7 stone 7. 'See,' I say defiantly, 'I told you I was 7$\frac{1}{2}$ stone. 'Are you sure?' says Editha, looking uncertainly at me and then back again at the scales, before leaving the room to report back to Dr Pinto.

'Okay, Claire, I really would like you to stay in hospital,' says Dr Pinto re-entering the room, 'but if you don't, at the present moment, I'm not going to stop you.' 'I've won,' I think to myself. 'However, I would like you to come here once a week to be weighed. If you don't you will be sectioned,' adds Dr

Pinto. 'Sure,' I say, a smile of victory flickering across my face. 'Whatever you say, doctor!' And with that I stalk out, triumphant.

———————

Mum and Dad can't believe that I haven't been taken into hospital, nor can Andy, and even Lorna's surprised. And me, I'm happy – I've been given the go-ahead to do what I like! I don't go back to work. Alone all day at home, with no one going on at me to eat, my obsessions and rituals run riot.

I wake at 5.15 a.m. after a broken night's sleep. Andy's still sleeping beside me. I pull at my stomach to check how big I am. I swing my legs over the side of the bed and try to stand, but my legs buckle beneath me and I sink softly to the floor. Shhh, mustn't wake Andy. I crawl out of the bedroom to the bathroom. My eyes fix nervously on the scales in the corner of the room, the harbinger of bad news. I make myself stand and walk unsteadily towards them. 'God, I wish I hadn't had that extra slice of cheese yesterday – 15 calories – what a pig! What happened to my control?' I think to myself as I slip out of my nightdress, take a deep breath and step onto the scales. My heart's pumping, too scared to look, yet dying to know. 'Yes!' I exclaim under my breath, 'I've done it, I've lost weight.' I rush over to the vanity unit and stare hard at my reflection. 'I've lost all this weight,' I think, 'but I look bigger; I'm fatter than ever.' I pinch my stomach hard, adding to the belt of purple bruises which sits permanently on my belly.

Andy's banging on the bathroom door. Quickly, I put on my nightdress. Got to cover myself up; I don't want him looking at me. While he takes a shower and gets ready for work, I hop on to the exercise bike for my five-mile bike ride. God, my legs feel like jelly, my pulse is racing, sweat pouring off me! 'Claire,' sighs Andy, 'get off that bloody bike.' I shoot him an evil look and pedal faster. 'That's it,' he says, 'I'm taking the pedals off when I get home tonight.' And with that he goes downstairs and slams out of the house. I slide from the bike to the floor. Time for stomach exercises. One, two, three, four...on and on I go, God I can't see, I'm blacking out. I shut my eyes tight. 'Fight the flab, you fat lazy bitch!' I scream. Exhausted, I lie prostrate on the floor. I open my eyes and the room swims back into focus. I don't stay lying down for long. Got to have another mirror check. I strip off my nightdress and examine my mirror image. 'I look bigger, I'm getting bigger!' I think. In a panic I run up and down the stairs five times as fast as I can.

I breakfast on two cups of coffee – black – and three cigarettes and then go back up to the bathroom to take a shower. Lying in the bath is painful: there's only a thin layer of skin to cushion my bones from the hard enamel. I take off my nightdress and force myself to look in the mirror. I run my fingers along my chest bones, twist round and count down my ribs through my see-through skin. I feel the nodules of my spine and grasp my protruding pelvic bones. My stomach is so hollow that if I lie down and press it I can feel my backbone. I put my hands round my waist until they almost join and feel slim, okay. As I glimpse the skeletal me I feel pure. But then all of a sudden I'm looking at a different picture; it's like someone's changed channels on a television. I'm fat again. I look like an onion, layer upon layer of lard. 'You disgusting fat bitch,' I say to myself, jumping into the shower and scrubbing at myself with the nailbrush until I am red raw. I'm trying to get rid of each layer of fat, each layer of me.

Out of the shower I hide my huge bulk in a long black skirt and a baggy jumper – even though it's midsummer. Then I make the bed – the duvet and pillows have to be just so; and start my daily routine of dusting, polishing, hoovering – think of all those calories I'm burning. After dinner – a Diet Coke – I think a brisk walk into town might do me some good. I'm feeling weak but the knowledge that I'm burning five calories a minute spurs me on. I'm compelled to stare at my ugly fat reflection in every shop window.

First stop is Boots for my famous cocktail of laxatives, diuretics and slimming tablets. Next it's the supermarket – to get something nice for Andy's tea. I wander up and down the aisles, picking up food. 'I want it,' I think, turning the bar of chocolate over in my hands. 'You can't have it,' says the voice in my head. Quickly I throw it back and wheel my trolley away. I see a man in the street scoffing a Cornish pasty. I am filled with guilt – it's like I'm eating it. I race home and shovel down laxatives.

When Andy comes home I present him with a mountain of a meal. I sit in another room and nibble at a slice of cheese. 'I ate earlier,' I say. Andy lets the lie linger between us. Poor Andy. I'm swallowing so many tablets, he says he can smell chemicals leaking from my skin. And I'm having to sleep on a towel because I am incontinent.

We go to Mum and Dad's for Sunday dinner. I hardly speak; I can't concentrate on conversation. I can't pretend any more. I eat some vegetables, safe in the knowledge that I have a stack of laxatives in my handbag at home. I can't wait to get back so I can swallow them. I daren't take them at Mum and Dad's. When I go to the bathroom, Dad's taken to standing outside the door and listening. I sing loudly, so he knows I'm not taking tablets or vomiting.

When Andy and I get home I go straight up to the bedroom to take my laxatives. I pull out the packets from the front pocket of my handbag – they are all empty. Bloody Andy! He's taken the tablets and put the boxes back! I'm not going to let him know it bothers me. I go downstairs and open the ironing board, whack the iron down on the rest and switch it on. I slam the iron on Andy's shirt, and run it briskly up and down the cotton. 'Where are they?' I spit. 'Where are what, Claire?' he replies, all innocence. 'You know,' I say, staring at him viciously. 'Give them to me you bastard, give them to me now!' 'Look at the state of you,' he says with disgust. 'You're a drug addict.' I put down the iron and push past him to the kitchen. I wrench open the cutlery drawer and grab the large carving knife with both hands. 'Give me my tablets,' I yell, advancing towards him. 'Give them to me now!' I lift the knife high and lunge. Andy grips both my arms and shakes me until I drop the knife. I sink to the floor sobbing. 'Please,' I cry, 'please, I have to have them, you know I have to have them, please.' 'Claire,' says Andy softly, taking me in his arms and holding me close, 'I just don't know what to do with you any more. This isn't Claire. This isn't you. What's happened to the girl I fell in love with? What's happened to the person who used to laugh and sing?

This is awful. Please Claire, please – you've got to go into hospital. If you don't go, the doctors are going to make you go eventually.' And I know he's right.

'Alright,' I say in an exhausted whisper, 'I'll go. But can I go on Tuesday? I can't face going tomorrow.' Relief floods Andy's face; he'll agree to anything. 'Course you can. I'll ring the hospital and let them know.'

Chapter nineteen

It's Monday. I'm frightened and angry. Everyone wants to make me fat and I can't have a big body. I have to be small.

After Andy leaves for work I go into town. I visit every chemist in Luton and buy pills at each one. I must have 1500 laxatives, 300 diuretics and several packets of slimming tablets. I hug myself – I'm carrying a bag full of treasure, and when I get home I'm going to bury it in the pockets of my clothes hanging in the wardrobe so Andy won't find it.

_____

'Good luck, I'll come to see you later,' says Andy on Tuesday morning, kissing me goodbye. His sister Diane stayed with us last night so she can drive me to hospital this morning. I know Diane likes to sleep in, so as soon as Andy leaves I get up and start to pack as quietly as I can so as not to wake her. I pinch a few of Andy's gym weights and his fishing weights and slip them under the lining of my bag. Then I hide my scales under my clothes. I need the scales so that I can check what I weigh and use Andy's weights to make myself heavier than I am.

I have a shower and get ready. I take the laxatives, diuretics and slimming tablets out of their packets, and tuck them into the body-stocking that I'm wearing. I lay strips of them around my front and back and even manage to wedge in a couple of bottles of diuretics. Then I put on a big jumper over the top. I'm taking my Carpenters cassette tapes with me, so I line the boxes with laxatives. I open my purse and fill every spare gap with tablets. I have a wad of cotton-wool pads and between each pad I fit four pills. By the time I've finished I'm a walking chemist.

'I don't suppose you remember me, Claire?' says Mike the nurse coming into the interview room on Ward 17. Of course I remember him, from my last stay in hospital. I look him up and down and then look away. He's another enemy. 'You know I've met you before,' I reply nastily. 'I'm going to be your keyworker and I'm here to help you during your stay in hospital,' Mike says. 'I don't want to stay here,' I spit back. 'Well, I'm going off duty now,' says Mike, 'bye.' 'That's right,' I yell after him, 'piss off!'

'Hi Claire.' It's Lorna. 'I've just got to search your bag,' she says. 'Do what you like,' I reply, listlessly. She roots through my holdall and fishes out the scales, which she confiscates. 'Okay,' she says, 'where are your laxatives?' 'I haven't any,' I reply. 'Claire,' she insists, 'you've been taking between 60 and 70 a day – I don't believe you haven't got any.' So I take 20 out of my purse and give them to her.

'No anorexic hands over 20 laxatives just like that,' she says. 'Where are the rest?' I turn away from her, and as I do, one of the pill bottles down my body-stocking rattles. Lorna grabs my jumper and lifts it up, staring at my armoury of tablets in horror. 'My God, Claire,' she says softly, 'you are so ill – and you can't see how ill you are.'

The following morning I get up early and start to drink huge amounts of water to increase my weight. I am due to be weighed. Lorna arrives. 'Andy rang this morning to say that some of his gym weights are missing,' she says. I don't reply. She searches the wardrobe, the locker, under the mattress, my holdall, my handbag. I pray silently that she'll miss some, but she finds nearly all of them. 'That wash-basin needs to be taken out of your room really – I'm not happy with it,' says Lorna, eyeing me knowingly. She leaves the room with the weights and I start to panic. I lift up the lining of my bag and find the remaining weights. I stuff the gym weights into my body stocking, and in desperation insert a one pound fishing weight made of lead into my vagina. It's painful but I'm prepared to do anything to cheat the scales; to stop them making me fat.

Ruby is weighing me. The scales say 7 stone 4, but I'm really under 6. Ruby escorts me to my case conference with Dr Pereira, Lorna and Sue the dietician. They tell me that things are going to get strict. I am to be weighed every day in my under-wear, and if I don't gain two pounds a week I will lose my privileges – it's the same old story. Sue wants to formulate an eating programme with my help; but I refuse to co-operate. 'What foods do you like, Claire?' asks Sue. 'None!' I scream, becoming hysterical. The meeting is terminated and Lorna takes me back to my room where I cry and cry and cry.

When I calm down a bit, I go downstairs to play the piano. Lorna comes in and sits beside me on the piano stool. 'Do you like crumpets?' she asks, gently. 'Yes,' I reply, 'I love crumpets; they're really nice with lots of butter.' 'If I buy you some crumpets,' she says, 'will you eat them?' 'I can't,' I say. 'Why can't you?' she asks gently. 'Because I don't deserve it,' I reply. 'Oh Claire, you do,' she says. 'You do deserve food. You're going to die if you don't eat.' 'I'd rather die,' I say. 'I don't like it here any more. I shouldn't have been born anyway.'

When my mum, my sister and Diane come to see me at visiting time I've worked myself up into a terrible state. 'Please take me away!' I cry. 'You can't let them keep me here. They're going to make me fat!' 'But there's nothing of you, Claire,' says Mum, trying to calm me down. 'You just don't want me to have a nice figure,' I scream, lifting up my top and pulling at my stomach. 'Look! Look at this. I'm fat, I'm fat, I'm fat!' I've never shown any of my family my body before, and naked horror fills their faces. Mum and Lisa start crying and Diane gulps and slaps her hand over her mouth as if she's about to throw up. Hearing the commotion, a nurse comes in and hurries my family from the room, but in a few moments I am chasing after them. 'Don't leave me here!' I scream, as they disappear round a corner. Two male nurses rush to restrain me. 'If you love me you won't leave me here,' I wail as the nurses battle to hold me. 'Don't leave me here!' I shout, twisting my head around, trying to catch a glimpse of my family. The nurses are dragging me back to my room, but I'm still screaming: 'I love you, I promise I'll eat, I'll promise I'll eat. Please take me home!'

Afterwards I sit huddled in the corner of my room. Lorna comes in. 'Claire, please try to eat; you've got to eat,' she says. I look her in the eye and say, 'I will die first before you make me put on a pound.' And I mean it. She tries to get me to take tranquillizers to calm me down, but I refuse – I don't know how many calories are in them.

'23rd July 1993,' I write in my diary, *'I haven't written for a few days as I feel like my whole world is being turned upside down. They have all got me now and I'm scared. I pray every night to God and beg him to make this all a dream, and that I wake up and people will leave me alone and I can carry on as I was. I have no control left, it is all being taken from me.*

Right now I wish I could die, then go to heaven and be loved, although I am not worthy of being loved – that I know. I'm ugly and nasty and, as people tell me, very selfish. Everybody says they care for me and love me but I don't feel like they do. I trust nobody, not even Andy, as they are all on at me and it's doing my head in.

I was so depressed this morning that I felt that my world was falling down around me. Lorna spoke to me and gave me a hug and it was as if she waved a magic wand and made all the pain go away. She is so lovely and kind. I trust her. She is the only person at this moment in time that I do, even though she goes on about wanting my true weight. I love her to bits, like a sister.

Dad brought my sandwich up at 5.00 p.m. It made me anxious as I do not usually get it until 7.00 p.m. He watched me so hard that I was unable to spit it out into a tissue.

By six o'clock I had severe stomach cramps and I knew then that my laxatives were starting to work, thanks be to God.

Andy was due up at 7.00 p.m. I made an excuse to Dad that I wanted a bath before Andy arrived, so Dad left, although he said that he thought I made myself sick after eating because I went to the toilet 10 minutes after. I telephoned Andy and said that I was taking a bath, so for him to come later. I had my bath which set my laxatives off early. I was in more pain than usual. My stomach is empty and cleansed now so it is worth it.

I felt so full of life after my bath – it was great. Andy arrived and I needed to get out of here so I persuaded him to take me to the hospital social club to see the band that was on. I lasted until 9.30 p.m. then I felt exhausted and Andy brought me back.'

I haven't eaten any hospital food for seven days. Mum and Dad bring me up a sandwich each night which I eat as little of as I can get away with. I am drinking massive amounts of water and Diet Coke, and every day the scales say something different. I'm finding it hard to concentrate and my vision is blurred. I have difficulty walking and severe pains in my chest, but I'm still secretly exercising in my room: I do sit-ups, star jumps and jog on the spot. I like the amazing control I have in hospital because there is no temptation to binge: there aren't cupboards full of food like there are at home. I feel high, like I'm separated from my body. I love that feeling – it's like being a spirit.

The only problem is I'm losing all my privileges. I've lost my single room and have to sleep in a dormitory which I hate; I'm not allowed off the ward and now they're threatening to stop my visitors. I'm going to have to do something. It's dinner-time. 'I'd like a cheese and onion sandwich,' I say to one of the nurses, 'but I don't want to eat it in front of the others. Can I have it in my room?' I am given permission to eat in my room, but I have to be supervised by a nurse.

Gradually I suss out the nurses, and ask those who are soft or stupid to sit with me. One of my regular nurses is Catherine, a student. She sits on my bed and talks to me while I have my sandwich. I break it into tiny bits, pick up each piece, pretend to eat it, swallow and throw it down my sleeve. 'You've done really well, Claire,' says Catherine, leaving the room. 'They must be daft to let a student observe me,' I laugh to myself.

As usual I am using laxatives in hospital. I ask other patients to buy them for me, or sneak out and buy them myself, using my Switch card. 'Dr So and So said it was okay for me to pop out,' I say to staff. I am a convincing liar, but sometimes I'm made to take Catherine with me. One day I ask another anorexic called Angie if she wants to come into town with us – Catherine won't have a hope in hell with two of us to look after. I say I want to go to the supermarket to buy ingredients for my sandwiches. 'You look tired. Why don't you sit down while I do my shopping?' I suggest to Angie, when we reach

Tesco in the Arndale Centre. Catherine doesn't know what to do – whether to come with me or sit with Angie. In the end she lets me go to Tesco while she and Angie sit on the seats outside. 'Don't buy anything low fat,' shouts Catherine as I disappear into the shop. Needless to say I buy skimmed milk and half-fat cheese.

With the food shopping done I turn to the real object of the trip – to get to Boots to buy laxatives. Boots is opposite Tesco, and as luck would have it a big fat man walks in front of me. Using him as a shield I scarper across to Boots. As I'm paying for my laxatives I see Catherine anxiously looking around for me. I grab two cans of drink and walk out of the shop saying, 'Look, I've bought you both a drink.' Catherine looks relieved. I chuckle to myself. I bet she's thinking, 'How sweet of Claire. I'm sure she hasn't been up to anything.'

As my meals aren't always monitored by inexperienced nurses, I am taking some food down. After three and a half weeks in hospital I start to look a little better. Friday the 13th of August is a hot day and I'm allowed to sit in the garden with Claire McCann who's come to visit. I feel the sun on my face and, for once, feel quite uplifted and positive about the future. After Claire leaves, my parents pop in. They've been on holiday in Tenerife and haven't seen me for two weeks. 'You're looking better, sweetheart,' says Dad. 'I'm really trying,' I tell them. 'I want to get well so I can be with Andy and we can start a family.' Relief lights their faces.

I have pasta for tea that evening and allow myself to swallow quite a bit. Suddenly I feel that I'm growing bigger. I've got to get rid of all this food. I go to the loo to vomit, but Editha follows and comes in with me. I'm in panic mode. 'Oh God,' I think inside the cubicle, 'I've got to shake her off.' I flush the toilet and come out of the cubicle. 'I'm just running to my room to get my cigarettes,' I breeze. I've got 160 laxatives hidden in my pillowcase. I rush to the room and push the door to. I seize the tablets and, because I'm in such a panic, ram the lot into my mouth, washing them down with Diet Coke.

I'm really tired and woozy. It's an hour later and I'm supposed to be going home for the evening – Andy's coming to pick me up. I'm scared about what I've done. I've never taken this many laxatives before. 'I don't feel so good,' I say to Andy, when he arrives. 'Can we just go to the hospital social club for a drink?' We walk to the club and I sit down heavily. 'Can I have a Diet Coke, Andy?' I say, fanning myself. I'm ever so hot now and finding it hard to catch my breath. My hands are tingling and the room is melting in front of my eyes. Sharp little pains are shooting up my arm and into my chest. Andy comes back with the drinks. I want to go to the loo. I try to stand, but my legs seem to have disappeared. I slither to the floor.

People gather round murmuring their concern; Andy collects me up like a bundle of washing. Half-running, half-walking, he carries me back to the Faringdon Wing and up the stairs to Ward 17, where I flop in a chair in the nurses' station. Barely conscious, I'm aware of Mike checking my blood pressure. Lorna walks in; she's been on duty on Ward 18 below – she's just popped up to see if Mike wants to go to the social club for a drink. 'What have you done, Claire – have you been exercising?' she asks firmly. 'No,' I slur sleepily, 'no I haven't.' 'What have you taken, Claire?' she demands urgently, feeling for my pulse. 'Tell me what you've taken.' 'Nothing,' I insist weakly. 'I haven't taken anything.' Lorna squats down and gives me one of her looks – her 'Lorna looks' I call them. 'What have you taken, *tell* me.' I can't lie to her. '160 Dulcolax,' I mumble. 'My God,' whispers Lorna, 'they are really fucking you up.'

'Mike!' Lorna yells, '160 Dulcolax – call an ambulance!' I am whisked to my room where Andy helps me into my nightdress. Lorna's told him that under no circumstances is he to allow me to sleep. 'Sing to me, Claire,' he says. 'Sing to me.' And I try. I sing 'Rainy Days and Mondays' by The Carpenters. There are tears in his eyes as I struggle to get the words out. I feel so ill and want to sleep, but I know I have to finish the song. Editha comes into the room and says, 'You're going to Casualty. We think you're going to go into shock.' 'You think she's going to have a heart attack, don't you?' murmurs Andy in disbelief. 'It's a big possibility,' says Editha; and I think 'Please God, let it happen. I can't cope with this any more.'

The ambulance crew arrive and I'm rushed by ambulance the short distance to Casualty, where a female doctor is waiting to see me. Andy's with me and so is Kathy, a night nurse from Ward 17.

I'm lying on a bed in a cubicle. Severe pain is ripping at my bowels which are boiling like an erupting volcano. My stomach starts to bloat out. 'My God,' I think, 'not only am I going to die, but I'm going to die fat!' 'Kathy!' I shout, 'I've got to go to the toilet.' She helps me to the loo, but when I get there I can't go. As I stagger back to the cubicle the pain intensifies and I collapse: I'm on the floor, vomiting, and my bowels begin to work. Someone throws me onto a commode. I collapse again. The doctor gets me back into bed and wires me up to an ECG to monitor my heart. 'We're going to have to put some drips through you,' she says. I'm horrified. 'What's in the drip?' I cry. 'What's in the drip?' 'It is fluid to replace what you are losing. Without it you will die,' she says matter-of-factly. 'It contains no calories,' she says, looking into my stricken face. 'Show me the bag,' I demand. She does, but even then I don't believe her.

Poor Mum and Dad. They've been called to the hospital to be told that I might die. They can't believe it – earlier in the day I'd been talking about having a baby, now I'm dying. Andy sits by my bed looking devastated; my brother Michael is pleading with me to live. Unable to move, with my family in tears around me, I pray 'Dear God, dear Jesus Christ, please let me die. My mind can't take this any more; I can't live with myself any more. Everyone'll be better off without me. I'm sorry for everything that I've done wrong. I know I'm bad, but please forgive me enough to let me die.'

By 2 a.m. I'm out of danger, and my family have gone home to bed. I'm starting to feel a bit better and I'm increasingly angry at being wired up to this drip. 'If you pull that out you will die,' says a night nurse called Denise, who catches me tugging at it. 'What are you pumping into me?' I demand. 'I can feel myself getting bigger.' Denise shows me the bag and says, 'Claire, it is just fluid to replace fluid you are losing.' Having pacified me a little, Denise sits and chats. 'I really want a cigarette,' I tell her. 'Come on then,' she says, conspiratorially. She pulls back the covers, helps me out of bed and shows me how to wheel my drip along beside me.

We reach the smoking room and Denise takes out her cigarettes. 'We had a young girl like you in here last year,' she says, lighting my cigarette. 'She was in the same bed as you. We all fought so hard to save her but we couldn't.' 'Veronica!' I think and go cold. 'Was her name Veronica?' I ask. 'I'm not allowed to say,' replies Denise. 'Answer me this then,' I insist. 'Was she 18 years old with blonde hair, and did she die just before Christmas?' 'Yes,' says Denise quietly. 'She was my friend,' I say thoughtfully. 'But I'm not like her,' I add. 'She was really thin and ill.' Denise puts her hands on my pelvic bones and shakes her head saying, 'I can't believe you can say there's a difference.'

Compared to Denise, the day nurses are horrible. 'And what did the anorexic eat for breakfast?' they say to each other in front of me. I hate that word. I can't even say it. 'I'm not an "anna"!' I yell at them. 'Don't call me an "anna"!' The other women patients on the ward aren't much better. They stand around my bed and say, 'God, you are so thin!', 'What's the matter with you?', 'How do you stand up?' I feel humiliated. I am also frustrated because I'm on bedrest and can't burn off any calories, and I'm bored because I don't have my tapes to listen to.

It's Saturday night. My eyes are still sore and gritty with dehydration, but I'm feeling better. I'm in a real panic about the drip though, and keep pinching the tube between my fingers to try to slow down the flow. 'I can't sleep – the drip's irritating me.' 'Can you take the drip out now, please?' On and on I go at the nurses. 'Will you ring the doctor now, please? The doctor said the drip could come out when I stopped going to the toilet and I'm not going any more.' I'm lying, but I kick up such a fuss that a doctor is called and the drip removed. The following day I'm transferred back to Ward 17.

I'm convinced that I'm going to lose my weekend leave because of the overdose. My brother's marrying Elaine on Saturday and I'm really scared that I won't be allowed to go to the wedding. 'Please let me go to my brother's wedding,' I say as I enter Dr Pereira's office. 'Take everything away from me. Lock me up for three days, I don't care; just let me go!' Dr Pereira calms me down. 'I'm not going to stop you going, Claire,' he says in his measured voice, 'but if you take laxatives again you will be confined to the Wing for five days.'

'I need to lose at least two stone – I'm never going to fit into my outfit for Michael's wedding,' I say to my keyworker Mike, adding, 'Can I go home and try it on?' 'Claire,' he replies, patiently, 'you know the programme doesn't allow you unplanned leave. And, anyway, your body image is so distorted, I don't think it'll do you any good.' 'I've been eating so much; I feel so big and bloated,' I say tearfully. 'Those feelings will become less intense as you get used to eating more,' Mike says, adding, 'The best thing is to tell us every time you get those feelings and we'll help you through it.' 'You don't want me to have a nice figure,' I whine. 'You're just trying to

make me fat.' 'Claire, you know that your programme is based on the Body Mass Index – your
weight gain targets are not going to make you fat.'

But the feelings won't go away. I'm up to my
usual tricks, and even pretend I'm constipated and
ask for an enema.

The night before Michael and Elaine's wedding,
Mum and Dad throw a barbecue for family and
friends. I feel like I don't fit in. I watch everybody
having fun and a few drinks, and feel like a freak. I
go into the kitchen where the food is laid out and
panic. I'm scared my control will snap and I'll end
up diving in like a pig. 'Go on, Claire,' encourages
Mum, 'it's Michael's wedding; have something to
eat.' I try to be normal. I pick up a paper plate and
dither at the table, trying to decide what to have.
Tentatively I choose a small bit of granary bread and
a piece of chicken. I start to eat; but then I feel really bad because I'm eating, and people can see me
eating and I don't deserve to eat. I put the plate
down on the table and push it away.

I wear lots of make-up for the wedding – I don't
want people to say I look pale. I've bought a black
and white suit and a big black hat. Before the
church service everyone's meeting in the pub.
'Claire, what are those two pieces of thread hanging
off your skirt?' says a friend of Mum's. As I reach
down to examine my hem she laughs and says,
'Your legs!'

'You're a selfish bitch – overdosing the week before your brother's wedding,' spits one of my
cousins. I don't reply. In a way it's what I want to
hear: someone else telling me I'm a bad person – my
self-hate's justified. 'God, Claire,' I think to myself,

'you are so vile – you don't deserve a family or friends. You don't deserve anything.'

After the church service there's a sit-down meal. I watch everybody enjoying their soup, their roast beef and potatoes. I'm feeling paranoid. I think people are watching me because they know that I have a problem. And I'm panicking because I don't know how many calories are in the food. I try to think back to my calorie book to work it out, and then get angry with myself for doing it. There are profiteroles for dessert. 'Stuff it,' I think, 'I'll have them.' I eat half a profiterole and put the rest under my spoon, even though I want it. Then I get angry with myself for being greedy, because I don't deserve anything nice.

Chapter twenty

My sister Lisa's been to visit me in hospital: she gave me a letter, and asked me to read it when she'd left.

———————

'There's only one way to describe my sister,' she writes, 'I used to say she's totally extraordinary: once you meet her you will never forget her. I'd always say this in a proud way.

You see, I used to watch the way she affected people around her. She drew people in with her liveliness and her conversation – always so interesting and humorous. She was the life and soul of any party. I would have given anything to be like her.

That was then. I don't mean to speak about her in the past tense, but it's the only way I can now. You see that person I just spoke about has been gone a long time. Now don't get me wrong, she hasn't died, but the person inside of her has – the one I admired and wanted to be so much like has gone as if she was never there in the first place.

If someone had asked me outright to fight for my

sister I would have and won, but it is so unfair. How do you fight your sister's mind? – God, I've tried. It's an impossible task. To describe my sister now, she lies on a bed day and night, watching the world go past, destroying herself slowly. Nothing to talk about apart from IT, nothing seems to matter to her, IT rules her life continually. Her life is going past day and night and is, no doubt, very lonely.

I don't give up easily. I don't want to be beaten, so that's why I'm writing to you. Please give me my sister back, the one I love so much. I can't keep fighting with you.

Come back soon Claire. I'll be waiting. Love always Lisa x'

Oh, I've got a lump in my throat! Her words mean so much. She's looked beyond my body, beyond my lies and manipulation. She sees my illness as a poisonous creeper which is choking the life out of her sister, not as part of me. Perhaps she's right, and perhaps I can find the strength to extricate myself and fight this illness. I sit on my bed, clutching the letter and crying my eyes out. But *how*?

'What would you like to do if you didn't have this illness?' asks Lorna at the group later that night. 'Your job,' I say without hesitation. The firmness with which I say it quite surprises me. 'And you'd be very good at it,' she replies, 'but you'd have to be well.' I don't know it yet, but Lorna's just handed me my weapon.

Towards the end of the evening Lorna shows me an article she's cut out from the *Daily Express*. 'What do you think of this picture?' she asks. The photograph is of an anorexic called Caraline and she's tiny. It says that she has an 11-inch waist. I'm jealous as hell: I want to be that small, I want to have that much control. 'She's really slim,' I say. 'Claire, she's dying,' replies Lorna gently. I don't say anything, but I take the article away with me.

Lying in bed that night I read Caraline's story. The article begins, '*Caraline weighs 3½ stone but still thinks she takes up too much space.*' I stop in my tracks. That's how I feel – that I take up too much space. I read on. Like me, Caraline has been sexually abused. Like me, she's been left feeling dirty and bad and that she doesn't deserve to live. I feel tremendous relief – I'm not alone, somebody else feels like me. Then something happens. I'm looking at her picture and my envy of her emaciated figure evaporates. 'This girl looks really *ill*,' I think to myself. I run my hands over my own skeletal frame and at last it dawns on me that I'm too thin. At last I realize that I'm killing myself for something that isn't my fault.

Just then Patsy, the patient in the bed next to mine, walks into the dormitory. She is mentally ill, deaf and dumb and we communicate in sign language. She's signing to me that it's time for my bedtime drink. Every night she brings me black coffee with two sweeteners, and every night she offers me a biscuit which I refuse. Tonight she has a packet of ginger nuts. 'Thank you,' I sign, and take three. I eat them and have no feelings of guilt – in fact I enjoy them. I've still got the body of an anorexic, but the combination of Lisa's letter and Caraline's article has somehow thrown a switch in my mind. I feel *so* different. As I settle down to sleep, an unfamiliar sense of peace runs through me. 'From now on,' I think to myself, 'everything's going to be okay.'

———————————

It's hard, but I've nearly finished my bowl of Alpen. 'Hi, Mum,' I grin. She's popped in on her way to work. She's surprised to see me eating at the dining table without a nurse watching me like a hawk. She sits down opposite me. 'I'm really going to get well,' I say. 'That's great, Claire,' she says, looking uncertain. Poor Mum; she's heard it so many times before. 'No, really!' I say. 'I've decided I want to set up a group like Lorna's.' 'Well, why don't you?' encourages Mum.

After the Alpen's finished and Mum's gone, I feel a little panicky, but the urge to get well seems greater than the urge to get rid of what I've just eaten. I talk through my feelings with Lorna and my anxiety passes. I'm able to eat my dinner and my tea. All the while I think about turning my illness around so I can help others, of using IT instead of IT using me.

Over the next week I put on weight and gain some privileges – I'm allowed two shopping trips and three overnight leaves at home. I have to stick to my programme when I'm at home though – in fact, Andy has to sign a menu-sheet to say that I have eaten all the food I'm supposed to. I am only allowed pasta with cheese and cheese sandwiches a maximum of three times a week: the idea is that I start to eat other foods, not just those I feel safe with. It's a struggle, and sometimes I sit on the kitchen step tearing my hair out. 'I can't do this,' I think, 'I feel so fat.' But there's a louder voice in my head saying, 'You can' and, for the most part, I do.

It's Tuesday 7th September. My weight is 8 stone 1, and it's a real weight, not a contrived one. I'm being discharged tonight although I will continue to see Ruby once a week and attend Lorna's group.

Andy's bought me a big bunch of flowers. I am so happy. 'I'm cured!' I trumpet to anyone who'll listen. Doubt flickers across their faces, and makes me angry. Part of me wants to say, 'You don't think I can get better, so I won't.' But a bigger part of me wants to be well.

It's frightening though, getting better. I've been living in a glass bubble, a spectator watching the world go by, but now I've smashed the glass I've got to participate. And the trouble is I don't know how. For 13 years I have been a bundle of obsessions and compulsions – anorexia personified. And if I'm not an anorexic, who am I?

With Lorna's help I'm finding out. Before, I felt so dirty and guilty about the abuse that I thought I didn't deserve to live, to take up space. Caraline's article made me realize that I was turning in on myself the anger I should have been feeling towards my abuser. Now I'm learning that I'm no different from everybody else – that I do take up space, that I need to nourish myself to live and deserve to do so. My self-loathing is beginning to dispel. I'm not saying I like myself, but I am getting to know and accept myself.

For years my illness controlled my personality; now I'm getting the upper hand and the real me is emerging. Little by little I am learning to voice my feelings instead of showing them through my body –

and it's a lot less painful. I am beginning to take an interest in things around me. I stop talking about food and weight – I never realized how much I went on about it – and people who once shied away talk back. My social life is improving and my confidence is growing. I am starting to laugh and feel happy, to sing and to mean it. 'You were so ill and withdrawn, always staring off into space,' comments Andrea at work. 'Now you're so different – it's like you've had a personality change.' My relationship with Mum and Dad is better. We are having less 'Have you eaten?' 'Am I fat?' conversations and more 'Have you heard about Mrs So and So round the corner?' chats. My periods come back – I'm over the moon. Now Andy and I can start a family.

I still have bad days though, when destructive thoughts circle my brain like ravening sharks. I'll want to purge, and sometimes I do. The difference is that immediately afterwards I'm not thrilled or relieved; instead I'm angry that I've failed. I'm fed up with all this. I've been doing it for years and it hasn't made me happy – now I want to stop. And now that I exist, now that I am a real person, I go and find someone to talk to about my feelings – because Lorna tells me that they matter, that I matter. I grit my teeth and keep my goal to help others fixed in my head. Somehow it's easier to get better for someone other than myself.

Little by little the good days seem to last longer, and soon I am way over my target weight – God, I'm *nine* stone! Lorna explains that after being so emaciated, the body will cling to every calorie. And that after a while, when the body realizes it isn't going to be starved any more, my weight will drop back and stabilize. Sure enough, it settles at about 8 stone 5.

'I owe you so much,' I tell Lorna. 'I couldn't have done this without you.' 'Claire,' she insists, 'it is your determination and insight into your illness which got you better. I could be the best nurse in the world, but if someone doesn't want to get well they won't.' But I find it hard to take any credit.

Chapter twenty-one

I've just read another article about Caraline in a women's magazine. She only agreed to be interviewed in the hope that she could stop other people dying of anorexia. I really want to get in contact with this girl – to tell her that she has made a difference. I don't suppose they'll pass the message on, but I'm ringing the magazine to explain that Caraline has helped save my life and that she needs to know. The girl at the magazine rings back and gives me Caraline's surname – Neville-Lister – and her address. Caraline wants me to write to her. I can't believe it. I'm writing her a letter, so I can post it today.

Caraline writes back by return of post, and pretty soon we are opening our hearts to one another on paper. 'It's a 24-hour fight every day to stay well,' I write. 'I do understand your fight,' she replies. 'You are showing remarkable bravery. Only to be admired.' I tell her about my dream to start a group for people with eating disorders, and that I have applied to the Eating Disorders Association asking to become a contact. Caraline writes back with encouragement.

As our friendship intensifies, we start to phone each other. Caraline has endless hope for me but none for herself. 'I wish I had had the chance of a nurse called Lorna,' she says, 'but it's too late. I'm going to die.' I find this hard to accept and very upsetting. 'Please don't be sad on account of me,' begs Caraline in her tiny, little girl's voice.

Caraline and I have arranged to meet. I take the train down to Brighton where she lives, and there she is waiting for me under the station clock. She's tiny, about five feet tall, with jet black hair which is cut short and gelled, huge blue-grey eyes and a wide smile. She's shrouded in layers of clothes, but her appearance is still attracting shocked looks from passers-by. Caraline is 29 but she weighs the same as a four-year-old. I hug her carefully, scared she might snap.

We go to a café where, over her cup of weak Marmite, she tells me about her terrible life. The eldest of seven children, she was sexually abused by her father, physically and mentally abused by her mother. After her father went to prison, her mother washed her hands of her children. They'd have one can of baked beans in a bowl between seven, or else their mother would chew a mouthful of beans, spit it back on the spoon and feed it to them. She beat Caraline and her siblings with the buckle-end of a belt. Locked in their rooms each night, with a bucket for a toilet, the children were so hungry they'd chew their candlewick bedspreads. Caraline became a mother to her sister and five brothers; she didn't attend school regularly and was always cleaning, washing and ironing. At 16, she started to control her eating – it was the only thing in her life that she could control.

Shunted from one special unit to another, she was force-fed and blackmailed into eating. 'You can read your sister's letter if you eat that potato,' they told her in one institution. In another she had no pillow – she had to earn one by putting on weight. She'd been sexually assaulted in one hospital, and told not to turn up at the accident and emergency department of another because her appearance distressed staff. In 10 years she earned the labels 'difficult', 'manipulative', 'beyond help'.

Now she's taken herself out of hospital and is living on her own. She eats nothing all day, and by five o'clock in the afternoon she's starving. Then she binges on cheese, pasta, scrambled eggs, bread, six bowls of cereal, cakes and custard. Sounds familiar? Then she throws up and takes laxatives; by the time she finishes it's 2 a.m. When she wakes up, her scales tell her there's not a flicker of a weight change.

She's very clear about why she does it. 'No one listened when I was a child, but now my scarred and wasted body says it all. I have to hold onto my "problem",' she explains, 'so my pain is understood, so it can be seen.'

———

'Dying to be slim?' I write in thick black felt pen. 'Do calories, food and weight control your mind?' I am making a poster advertising my self-help group – Andy's going to photocopy it at work and I'm going to spend my day-off sticking posters up around the town – on buses, on lamp posts, in the library, at the Citizens' Advice Bureau. Meeting Caraline has made me even more determined to put my own experience of eating disorders to good use.

'There aren't enough Lornas around, and people need to know that this isn't about slimming, that it goes much deeper than that,' she tells me, adding 'Doctors need to learn from people like you – someone who knows what it feels like and who understands. They need to know that brutal treatment just doesn't work. The professionals never listened to me; perhaps they'll listen to you.' 'Caraline,' I promise, 'I'll make them listen, and as long as I am alive, people will speak your name.'

I've been to the church Veronica used to attend, and told them about my plan to set up a self-help group. They remember Veronica and are only too pleased to let me use a room in the church hall for free. 'There is a self-help group being held at the Holy Ghost Church hall, Luton on 4th February 1994,' I write at the bottom of my poster, adding my phone number. I don't realize till later that 4th February is the date Karen Carpenter died.

The EDA have rung me a few times and I've sent them some more information about myself. Even if they don't accept me as an official contact, I'm going to start a self-help group anyway. It's the first meeting tonight, and I'm planning to run it along the lines of Lorna's group. I'm really excited – nervous in case nobody turns up, nervous in case they do. Caraline's sent me a lucky mascot doll made of beads, which I'm going to take along in my handbag. I'm at Radio Rentals when a lady from the EDA rings. 'Do you still want to start a self-help group?' she asks. 'Well, actually,' I reply, 'I'm holding my first group tonight.' 'Well, congratulations,' she says, 'you've been accepted as an EDA contact and we will be recommending you to sufferers in your area.'

I am walking towards the Holy Ghost Church hall and there are two people waiting outside. I show them into the room set aside for us and take a deep breath. 'My name's Claire, and this time last year I was in a psychiatric wing suffering from anorexia nervosa. I know what you are going through and how important it is for people to talk. And I promise that during the hour and a half a week that we spend together, you will be understood.'

The following week a journalist from *Luton on Sunday* makes contact. She's seen my posters and comes to interview me. A week after her piece appears eight people turn up to the group and then the phone starts ringing. I'm racing about like a blue-arsed fly: I'm doing the group every Friday, studying for my BTEC Continuing Education Higher Certificate of Counselling at night school every Thursday, taking calls from sufferers in the evenings and working at Radio Rentals full-time! I'm not sure that Andy likes the new me. He seems distant; he's spending more and more time at his mum's. He's only known me with anorexia, and sometimes I wonder whether he loves the recovered Claire.

———————

Caraline's asked me to go down to Brighton again to see her. 'I'll meet you under the station clock, Linda,' she says. She's taken to calling me Linda because she thinks I look like Linda Nolan. Caraline's shivering in a large black fluffy cardigan, a grey T-shirt and a pair of black leggings held up by a pair of braces. She's deteriorated a lot. I'm devastated. I plaster a brave smile to my face and scoop her up in a bear-hug. She's just a bundle of bones, a starving little sparrow.

It's weird because neither of us likes having our photo taken, but we've both brought cameras. Perhaps we know that this will be the last time we'll meet. Caraline wants to get out of Brighton for the day and directs me to a waiting train. As she struggles aboard I'm terrified that she's going to fall. She's so unsteady and so slight, she could easily slip down the gap between train and platform.

I sit opposite her in the carriage; her seat seems to be swallowing her up. 'Come and sit next to me, Claire,' she says weakly. I cross to the seat beside her and take her hand. She's talking and having trouble keeping her eyes open. Suddenly they close and her hand goes limp. I freeze. 'Oh my God,' I think, 'she's dead!' I'm staring at her face and thinking, 'We're on this train and I don't know where we're going, and she's dead!' I'm just about to open my mouth and call for help, when Caraline stirs. 'Don't worry, I love you too much to die on you yet,' she smiles, reading my mind.

We get off the train at Lewes, two stops from Brighton. It's cold and we have to keep stopping for Caraline to catch her breath. We go to a pub and accost strangers to take photographs of us with our arms round each other, smiling. My smile cracks, and I begin to cry for the friend I know I'm going to lose. 'Don't cry, Claire,' says Caraline, 'we are closer than friends, closer than sisters and our relationship goes beyond the grave. I'll always be with you.' She laughs, 'If I have to pay God 50,000 pounds I'll come back and rattle a few pictures or something to show you I'm there.'

'Will you do one final thing for me?' asks Caraline on the train back to Brighton. 'Name it,' I reply.

'I feel too weak to prepare my food. Would you do it?' She's talking about her binge food. The girl's in torment; I'm not going to refuse. She takes me into her local supermarket and then disappears among the aisles. At first I don't worry. I find some miniature cakes with 'Forever Friends' written on top in pink icing. I want to buy one for Caraline. I know if she eats it she'll throw it up, but I want her to have some food associated with love. 'Where the hell is Caraline?' I think as I pay for the cake. Frantically I start to scan the shop. I'm worried now, terrified Caraline's collapsed. I race up and down the aisles, scared as a mother whose toddler's wandered off. Then I catch sight of her queuing at one of the tills and breathe a sigh of relief.

'I've got you something,' I say to Caraline, getting out the little cake. She bursts out laughing, digs into her shopping bag and fishes out an identical cake. 'And this is for you!' she exclaims.

Back at her flat, I put potatoes in the oven to bake, fill saucepans with water ready for pasta, slice a whole loaf of crusty bread, grate two large blocks of cheese and open all the tins.

'I've got something else for you,' says Caraline, coming into the kitchen. She's hiding something under her jacket. 'Squeeze,' she says, indicating something in the crook of her arm. I squeeze and hear a little 'miaow'. 'How the hell am I going to get a kitten home on the train?' I am thinking, when Caraline laughs and brings out a white toy cat. 'I'd like you to have her,' she says. 'Her name's Bess. And I want you to have Boots my teddy bear – and my scales.' She knows she won't be needing them much longer. She also gives me a book about the treatment of anorexia: the pages are peppered with Caraline's abusive annotations.

It's a quarter past five. I have to go. 'I'll walk with you as far as the sweet shop, Linda,' says Caraline, packing the things she's given me into a carrier bag. At the shop we embrace. I wrap my arms around her and she nestles into them like a baby. 'I love you, Caraline,' I say. 'I love you too,' she replies. And it's hard to say goodbye because we both know it's goodbye forever. Then she turns and disappears into the sweet shop to buy chocolate for her binge.

On the train I look at the carrier filled with Caraline's life and the little cake she gave me, and cry all the way home.

'You just can't do this,' I tell Caraline on the phone that night. 'You can't just die. I want you here.' 'Claire,' she replies gently,' 'you've got to let me go.' 'I can't, Caraline. Please, I don't want you to die,' I say sobbing. 'If I'd met you two years ago you really would have helped and you have helped, but it's too late,' she says. 'It doesn't have to be,' I beg. 'Claire, you've got to let me go,' she replies. 'I know,' I whisper, 'I know.'

Two weeks later the answerphone's flashing. Andy's gone round to have tea at his mum's. I kick off my shoes and press 'Play'. 'Claire,' says the tinny machine, 'it's Judy, Caraline's friend.' I freeze. 'Don't be upset,' she continues, 'Caraline has had a peaceful release.' 'Caraline! Caraline!,' I'm racing round the house, screaming her name. I knew it was going to happen but I can't bear that it has. 'Caraline! Why did you have to leave me?' I cry. By the time Andy gets home I am a sobbing wreck – he can do nothing to comfort me.

'Why did you have to die? You were such a beautiful person – it should have been me who died, not you,' I wail at the walls. I can't work, can't do the group, can't sleep, can't eat. I'm spiralling out of control. I'm back on the laxatives. I lose 18 pounds in one week. I'm in danger of losing everything and I don't care. I idolized Caraline, and being without her is horrific.

Three weeks after Caraline's death I find a letter on the doormat. It looks like Caraline's writing on the envelope. I rip it open and inside find a single sheet of lined A4. 'Dear Linda Nolan – oops! Claire,' it says. It's a short note, unsigned and undated, but unmistakably from Caraline. She touches on our last day together and finishes, 'Please Claire, please be my voice, don't let me die for no reason.' I look at the postmark on the envelope: it's smudged, illegible. I laugh out loud. 'Okay sweetheart!' I say, 'I get the message: I won't let you down!'

Epilogue

I went on to name my self-help group 'Caraline' in
memory of my friend. Having passed my BTEC Continuing Education Higher Certificate of Counselling,
I began counselling anorexics, bulimics and compulsive over-eaters; and in September 1994 I was
awarded the Whitbread Young Volunteer of the Year
Award by HRH Princess Michael of Kent for my
work in the community. I went on to appear on television, was interviewed by national newspaper and
magazine journalists, and even gave a talk to psychiatrists at St George's Hospital in London.

In April 1995 'Caraline' was granted funds by
Bedfordshire Health and Bedfordshire County Council and the service began to grow. I was able to give
up my job at Radio Rentals to run the self-help
group and counselling service full-time. Our clients
are all ages, and include young children and middle-
aged men. It is our aim to counsel and support sufferers in the community; hospitalization is a last
resort. We have heard of people mortgaging their
homes to send their suffering relatives to expensive

private clinics and hospitals in this country and abroad. To treat each client it costs us just a small fraction of the fees such places charge. We offer a weekly self-help group for sufferers, one-to-one counselling sessions and specialized eating programmes. Once a month we have a carers' meeting where, without breaking client-confidentiality, we offer carers support and advice on how to manage at home. Carers and sufferers also have access to a telephone helpline.

There is a common misconception that anorexia nervosa is just a diet which got out of hand. But an eating disorder is not a slimmer's disease; rather it is the symptom of stress or other profound emotional damage or psychological problems. About one third of sufferers have been sexually abused; others may have been physically or mentally abused. Eating disorders can stem from the fracture of a family through divorce or death, the break-up of a relationship, conflict over sexuality, bullying or pressure to achieve. There is a great deal in the press about the detrimental influence of emaciated models on young girls. Personally, I don't believe that seeing images of skinny women gives you an eating disorder – I think there are usually other factors involved. That said, I don't think the portrayal of women in the media helps matters. Film stars like Kate Winslet tell how they have been asked by movie directors to lose weight, even though they are not medically overweight. In the modelling world normal-sized women are often shunned in favour of those who are impossibly thin, be it naturally so or otherwise. The message is that being thin equals happiness and success. And those with a very low self-esteem might think that the answer to their problems lies in trying to emulate the women who are being presented as the ideal.

The earlier an eating disorder is caught the better the prognosis, and to this end 'Caraline' undertakes to give educational presentations to doctors, nurses, social workers and teachers. I kept my promise to my friend – the professionals are listening and speaking her name. Figures show that 10 per cent of sufferers die either from the effects of starvation or by committing suicide. Since 'Caraline' has been in existence, we have not seen one of our clients die.

1996 saw 'Caraline' gain charity status and receive a grant from the National Lottery Charities Board. The charity's patrons now include Claire Rayner OBE, Dame Cleo Laine, Diane Youdale, Derek Prag (a former Member of the European Parliament), Dr Roger Hood (a senior director with KPMG Management Consultants) and none other than Dr Robin Pinto, who treated me in the Faringdon Wing.

Our service is currently limited to the Bedfordshire area, but we receive calls on the helpline from all over the UK, and from Europe and America. My dream is to make 'Caraline' a national, if not an international, charity.

On a personal note, my marriage to Andy, sadly, did not survive. In the summer of 1995 I began to have counselling for the sexual abuse which blighted my life. With the on-going help of my wonderful counsellor Brenda Isles I am finally closing the door on that chapter of my life. I would be lying if I said I didn't have the odd anorexic thought; but I now understand why those thoughts happen and how to deal with them. When I first started 'Caraline', I kept myself well for other people; now I can honestly say I do it for me.

Claire Beeken 1997

My Continuing Journey to Wholeness

After *My Body, My Enemy* was first published in April 1997, 'Caraline' went berserk: the phone never stopped ringing – calls to our helpline increased by 130 per cent, and I received mail from all over the world. I was interviewed by The Daily Telegraph and The Express, and appeared on Sky Television. When the book went on to be translated into German, Dutch, Norwegian, Japanese and Danish, even more interest was generated. Calls and letters continue to pour in from sufferers seeking help or saying how much the book has helped them; and from mental health professionals seeking advice or wanting to refer clients to us.

One such call was from a Danish social worker called Jan who worked for a publicly funded psychiatric unit called Trehoje Plejehjem in Vildbjerg. Jan had read the book, and wanted my advice about a client of his who had suffered from anorexia for more than 10 years. I readily gave him some suggestions over the phone and thought no more about it.

Then I had another phone call from Jan. A team

of medical professionals from the psychiatric unit wanted to fly to England to find out more about 'Caraline'. Theirs wasn't a unit specializing in eating disorders; in fact, they had just the one anorexic patient. I welcomed the idea, but warned that we had only one counselling room. I was concerned that these people were going to fly all the way over and think they were going to see this amazing clinic, and that I was some sort of professor of eating disorders – which simply isn't the case! So I explained that 'Caraline' occupied two rooms above a solicitor's office – one we used as a clerical office, the other as our counselling room. But the Danes didn't seem put off by this, and in June 1998 Jan came over for three days, together with Jens, the director of the unit, and Maja, a clinical manager.

During their visit Jan, Jens and Maja sat in on some client counselling sessions, and attended our weekly self-help group. Anorexics, bulimics and compulsive over-eaters spoke about their treatment and how 'Caraline' had helped them. I also showed our Danish visitors round the new in-patient mental health units that have replaced the Faringdon Wing – Townsend Court and Oakley Court. They don't look like mental health units – the outside walls are painted in bright colours, and there are no dormitories; everybody has a single room. The approach to eating disorder clients is more client-centred now – sufferers are encouraged to make up their own goals and set up their own privilege systems.

At the end of their trip Jan, Jens and Maja all said their visit to 'Caraline' had made a remarkable impression, and that they were going to make quite a few changes at their own unit. They said that by watching us at work they had learnt how important it is to show compassion and understanding to clients. I think it says a tremendous amount about the Danish health service that they sent over three people on a fact-finding mission to England in a bid to help just one patient. Before they returned home, Jan asked if I would consider travelling to Denmark. 'Sure', I said, never dreaming that the trip would actually come off. In the short-term I had rather more pressing concerns: we desperately needed new office space.

It had got to the point where 25 Upper George Street had come to the end of its life – it was just too small. We were inundated with clients. The number of people attending the self-help group had increased by 84 per cent. Sometimes the room wouldn't hold all the people who came, and we would run out of chairs! We had a huge amount of counselling to do, and only one room to do it in. Something had to be done.

In early 1998 we began to look around for bigger offices with the help of commercial property agent Stephen Wood. 13 George Street West was a complete wreck. I looked round with 'Caraline's' Chairperson John Butler, Harry Kline our Honorary Fundraiser and Stephen. It was a four storey Victorian listed building that hadn't been occupied since the seventies. We had to enter the building through a back entrance because the front door was boarded up. Half the staircase was missing, and to get into one room you had to crawl through a little hole in the wall. The building was a mess, but I knew as soon as I walked in that this was it; this was what I wanted for 'Caraline'. Over the next few weeks Harry and I looked round other properties, but I wasn't interested – I wouldn't consider anything else.

Harry met up with the owner of the building Nick Hill, a Harley-Davidson-riding property developer. He'd bought the building many years ago, and owned the two properties next to it. When he heard that we were a charity, he very kindly said that he would sell to us for just under £100,000, well below the market rate. And, what's more, he would totally refurbish and decorate the building to our specifications! His only proviso was that we allow people interested in his other buildings, to come and see his handiwork. We were thrilled, but where was this £100,000 going to come from?

We decided to approach the National Lottery Charities Board. We'd already had one slice of money from the Lottery, and didn't know whether we'd get another; but you've got to try, haven't you? I am a firm believer in fate, and felt sure if we didn't get the money from the Lottery something would turn up.

On a cold windy February day in 1999 a woman called Wendy Cooke from the National Lottery Charities Board came to see us. She met Harry Kline, John Butler and me at the current 'Caraline' offices for what turned out to be a gruelling three-hour interview. We took her on a tour of 13 George Street West. I was so keen for her to see the potential of the place. I jabbered on about our plans and pushed her through the little hole to the otherwise inaccessible room. Then she said she was pregnant, and I thought, 'Oh no, what have I done to the poor woman?'

Back at the office, she got down to brass tacks. She got a stack of papers out of her bag and said briskly, 'We really can't go off at a tangent here because I've got an awful lot to ask you.' In other words, don't waffle! No stone was left unturned, and rightly so, but some of her questions really threw me. 'Who buys the milk in the morning?' she asked. 'Err, I do,' I stuttered, wondering if it was a trick question. There was a strict air about Wendy, and I really felt that if I answered a question wrong, it would be a case of go straight to Jail, do not pass Go, do not collect £200, or in this case £100,000!

Wendy did not give anything away. By the end of the interview my head was pounding and I had no idea whether we had even a hope of securing a grant from the National Lottery Charities Board. John and Harry, who are generally so optimistic, felt the same. Even Harry's usual charm met with a brick wall: Wendy refused to allow him to walk her down the stairs – perhaps escorting someone to the front door might be deemed a bribe! I suppose assessors like Wendy have to be seen to be completely impartial, and rightly so; but it did make for an incredibly stressful three hours.

We did not hear anything until April. It was my birthday; I had an awful chest infection and was round at my mum's for tea and sympathy. The phone rang and it was Harry. 'Claire,' he said in a dull voice, 'I've got some news.' 'Oh, yeah,' I replied, bracing myself for some of the bad variety. 'I'm afraid to say,' he began, 'the Lottery have agreed to give us funding!' I just screamed, 'Oh, my God!' I told Mum who was really happy for me, and we rang Dad; in fact I think I rang everybody I knew in the world. 'What timing,' I thought, 'What a fantastic birthday present!'

Nick Hill was as good as his word, and renovated the property just how we wanted. There are four counselling rooms, a large group/training room, an office; and disabled access at the rear of the building. Many original features have been retained: there is a little fireplace in one of the counselling rooms, and a huge fireplace with a stunning marble surround in the office. With the help of my staff, I chose the carpets and colour schemes, and the place is full of warm yellows and calming lilacs. It looks how I imagine a private clinic in Harley Street to be. In fact it is so much more than an office building, we decided to call it a centre!

We moved in September 1999, and the following month Tim Ellis from the National Lottery Charities Board officially opened the building at a reception attended by over 30 distinguished guests. They were representatives from the local Community Health Care Trust, local voluntary services, HarperCollins publishers, the people who helped with the centre's acquisition and renovation, as well as trustees, staff and users of 'Caraline'.

We named the new centre Kline House, after Harry Kline our sterling Honorary Fundraiser and a trustee of 'Caraline'. You can't not like Harry. Now 82 and a widower, he has worked tirelessly for 'Caraline' since he got the bit between his teeth in 1995, after a friend told him about our charity. His dogged determination tempered with a gentle humour makes him unstoppable! He has nursed us through two Lottery applications and it is mainly down to him that we got such a great deal on our building. It was no great surprise to those of us who are privileged to work with Harry, to discover that he was honoured with the Military Cross for bravery in Italy during World War II, and with the MBE for his work restoring public utilities during the Suez crisis in 1956.

Harry, bless him, is very quick to give my book to anybody who gets involved, even if we are paying them. He gave a copy to Stephen Wood, the property agent who showed us around George Street West. A week later, Stephen turned up to have a chat with me. 'I read your book,' he said, 'And I'd really like to help in some way.' When you work for a charity, these words are music to the ears. So we took him up on his offer and made him a trustee.

We have a strong management committee – members come from different walks of life and bring the benefit of their various strengths and past experiences to the charity. Our trustees include Mark Agius, a former GP who is now the local Community Trust's medical adviser, Sean Sidhu-Brar, a barrister who used to work as a mental health nurse and Linda Newcomen, a saleswoman, who is also our Carer Representative. Our wonderfully efficient Honorary Secretary Sam Hillyard, also does voluntary work for the Association of Cystic Fibrosis Adults, and our Honorary Auditor Duncan McPherson works for KPMG. My dad John is both a trustee of 'Caraline' and our Honorary Accountant. When I started 'Caraline', Dad taught himself accounting and all about computers so he could get to grips with our finances. He works full-time for Vauxhall and spends every spare minute number-crunching for 'Caraline' – I cannot thank him enough. There are so many other people who deserve a huge thank you: my dedicated team of staff and volunteers – Staci McPherson, Joy Simpson, Imelda Flanagan, Chris Wise, Barbara Marten-Hale, Amanda Ward and Deborah Meddes; also, Gerald Pearce and Carolyn Marshall, my counselling supervisors, Carrie Roberts, my college tutor and Jayne Hodgson, a special friend.

I owe a great debt of thanks to John Butler, who is Honorary Chairperson and also a trustee of 'Caraline'. I met John, a softly spoken Lancashire lad in his early thirties, in 1994, the year I started 'Caraline'. He was managing Beacon House, the Community Mental Health Centre in Dunstable, and I approached him about using one of its counselling rooms. When 'Caraline' was granted funding by Bedfordshire Health and Bedfordshire County Council, I realized that the charity needed a management committee since public money was coming into the equation. I asked John to become our Chairperson, and he has been juggling his work for 'Caraline' around his busy career ever since.

I really don't know how he does it. As well as managing Beacon House, he works as a Community Mental Health Nurse and a Research Nurse. Somehow, he still has time to contribute to mental health publications, and gain an MSc in Mental Health Studies. He also trains mental health professionals, principally in cognitive behavioural therapy. I might be the public face of 'Caraline', but it is John who maintains the nuts and bolts that keep the structure of the charity together. He wrote the constitution, and it is he who submits the incredibly complex applications for funding that enable us to function. Not only that, he offers cognitive behavioural therapy to 'Caraline' clients as well.

Securing funds to keep the charity working is an uphill struggle, and I think it always will be. We're okay for this year, but funding will tail off over the next couple of years. Our joint finance from Bedfordshire Health and Bedfordshire County Council is on a reducing scale, which effectively means that in three or four years time we will have no money to carry on, and will have to look for funding from other sources. We also always need volunteers – to man the helpline, do support work, fund-raise: there are loads of ways for people to get involved.

In April 1999 the proposed trip to Denmark became reality. The Danes covered my airfares and accommodation and so, still recovering from my chest infection, I found myself on a plane to Billund airport. The infection had really knocked the stuffing out of me; I'd lost weight and didn't look at all well. I was concerned that people would think I still had an eating disorder. Maja, Jan and Jens met me at the airport. It was really nice to see them again and they made me feel very welcome. We drove through the flat countryside to the huge house where I was booked in for bed and breakfast, and then to the unit where we were to have lunch. My other worry was the food. I knew that the Danes ate a lot of fish and I hate fish. 'I can't say that I don't like it,' I thought, 'They'll take one look at me and think that I really am ill.' So I said I was allergic to it. 'What do you like?' Jan asked. 'Oh, chicken, mashed potatoes, things like that,' I replied. And everywhere I went, that's what I was given – chicken and mash!

Trehoje Plejehjem was a huge bungalow, surrounded by beautiful gardens. There were wide hallways, plate glass windows overlooking beautiful gardens and paintings everywhere. The unit was home to all sorts of people with long-term health problems – some had been there 10 or 15 years. And it really was a home. Each room was like a self-contained studio flat. Clients had their own bathroom, a little stove and patio doors opening on to the garden. Staff didn't just enter a room, they knocked and had to be invited in:

they would almost always be offered tea. I drank buckets of tea while I was there!

I was moved by the dedication of the Danish health care professionals. Although I could not understand the conversations between the clients and the professionals, the body language spoke volumes. It was a very caring place, where people had a genuine regard for their fellow human beings. I felt that we as a country could learn a great deal from the Danes in their treatment of eating disorders, and actually questioned the need for me to be there!

During my three-day stay I saw the client that Jan had originally contacted me about. She seemed to get a boost from my visit, and her mother was kind enough to invite me to their home for dinner. The client came too – it was the first time in years that she'd eaten at home with her parents. You could tell her mum had been cooking all day – everything was homemade, right down to the after-dinner biscuits. The mother couldn't speak English and we communicated through Jan. 'I can't believe Claire Beeken is sitting at my table,' she said. 'I'm honoured to be here,' I replied. And she cried.

The following evening I delivered a lecture to sufferers, and medical and mental health professionals from all over Denmark. The evening was arranged by Trehoje Plejehjem, and a hundred or so people paid about £4.50 each to the unit to hear me speak. This was rather daunting to say the least! I was really nervous. Not only did I have a chronic cough left over from my chest infection, I also had to speak through a hired interpreter. He was a middle-aged man called John. 'I don't want to be silly about this,' he said when we met, 'but I have to tell you that I read your book and I found it amazing, so moving...'. With that, his voice broke and he began to cry. He went on, 'And you are here now and it is such a privilege to work with you.' I was taken aback, and very touched.

The lecture was nerve-wracking. The press were there, and I was due to speak for two hours. I began by telling the audience a bit about my story and went on to talk about 'Caraline', what we did and hoped to achieve in the future. I wanted to impress upon people that my treatment isn't a magical cure – it just seems to be working for us. I had to remember to pause for long enough to let John translate my words, and my cough was bothering me. I'd managed to find a pharmacist and bought some cough medicine, but I still had to keep swallowing water to try to stifle my splutters. I would cough, drink some water and then try to remember to stop at natural pauses in my lecture, but John had to ask me to repeat myself several times.

'What the hell am I doing?', I thought at one point. 'How the hell have I got myself here, so many miles away from home, talking to people who can't understand a word I'm saying!'. I had to be really careful not to use slang because John couldn't interpret phrases like 'going for a fag'. And it was hard to convey to the audience how little I had weighed during my illness. They all work in kilos; I only know stones. I stood there for what seemed a lifetime, trying to work out how many stones were in a kilo. In the end my maths gave up on me, and I used the space between my finger and thumb to indicate that I had been very very small indeed!

After my lecture I answered questions. Some medical professionals don't particularly like counsellors and I was prepared for some tricky questions, but there were none. Everyone was eager to learn and very appreciative. In fact when it was all over, people were asking me to autograph their copies of *My Body, My Enemy*, and those who didn't have books, handed me scraps of paper to sign. It was completely overwhelming.

Sadly, eating disorders, like drug abuse, are as common in countries like Denmark as they are in our country. Since the book was published we have seen more high-profile people such as Tracy Shaw, the Coronation Street star, admit to past problems with food. The very fact that I am adding these chapters for a new edition of *My Body, My Enemy* proves that there are too many women, and indeed men, suffering from eating disorders. I am very pleased that 'Caraline' has been provisionally approved as a training centre by the Associated Examining Board to offer Central School for Counselling Training short courses and certificates in counselling, theory and skills. The large training/group room we have in the new building is perfect for lecturing. It is gratifying to know that we at 'Caraline' can teach more people to care for those with eating disorders.

People develop eating disorders for all sorts of reasons, and there is no set pattern for recovery. I am very grateful to former clients Rebecca and Staci, who have allowed me to document their stories.

Rebecca was just about to have her 15th birthday when she contacted 'Caraline'. She came to see me with her schoolteacher. Rebecca was bulimic, and had confided in her teacher. The teacher had read my book and lent it to Rebecca. Rebecca was shy, and it was hard work trying to get her to speak. When she did talk, I discovered her mum and dad had broken up, and that her mum had a new partner and baby. Rebecca had been devastated when her father left and, although she felt very close to the baby, I think all the turbulence in her young life had made her insecure.

Rebecca was also self-harming with a razor blade. She showed me her arms – I was horrified; she'd really scarred herself. She said she felt in so much pain and cutting herself was the only way she could think of to make it go away. I explained to her that at 'Caraline', we can only help with eating disorders; we are not qualified to look after people who are harming themselves. So she took herself off to a psychologist, but also came to our weekly self-help group.

Once she'd stopped self-harming, we were able to begin counselling. Like all 'Caraline' clients, Rebecca followed an eating plan. I asked her to make three different lists. A: A list of foods that she liked and felt safe eating. B: A list of foods she genuinely disliked: it wouldn't matter if she had an eating disorder or not. C: Foods she would like to eat but did not allow herself. Like most bulimics Rebecca's list included carbohydrates like crisps and chocolate. They were the 'trigger' foods that often led her to binge and therefore vomit.

Of course we all crave what we deprive ourselves of and, when a bulimic eats a piece of chocolate, she thinks, 'Well, that's it, I've blown it. I may as well eat the whole lot now.' Because they feel they have relented and eaten what they see as a 'bad' or 'unsafe' food, they go on to binge and vomit. So when we devise an eating plan with a client, we incorporate some of the foods on List C. This way the client won't just restrict herself to the foods on List A. The eating plan gives her permission to have a few crisps or a bar of chocolate, and she will realize that they needn't be 'bad' or 'unsafe'. The eating plan encourages a client to develop a healthier relationship with food.

To help clients manage their eating plan, they keep a food diary – an idea I got from an eating disorder conference that I attended at St George's Hospital in London. I show each client how to draw up a diary with columns headed DATE, DAY, TIME, QUANTITY, FOOD, DRINK, BINGE, VOMIT. Opposite is a space for THOUGHTS, FEELINGS & EMOTIONS. The client writes out all the meals and snacks for the following day. When they get up in the morning they look at the plan and try to follow it, filling out the details in the various columns. Hopefully at the end of each day, there will be two matching entries. To help the client focus on the plan, and the counsellor to assess how much progress is being made, the client fills out how they are feeling on the THOUGHTS, FEELINGS & EMOTIONS page, and also whether they felt the need to binge or vomit.

Rebecca and I worked hard together over the next three years, and I distinctly remember the session where we made a real breakthrough. I thought that it might help to take the pressure off her and put the onus on a puppet. I haven't any puppets, so I grabbed a paper bag and called it Laurie. Rebecca had a Clinton Cards paper bag, so she said her puppet's name was Clinton, which I thought was clever. My aim was to talk through the puppets, and then get her to own what her puppet was saying. Rebecca's puppet went very limp and Laurie said, 'Clinton looks really sad'. 'He is sad,' said Rebecca. 'Why are you sad, Clinton?' asked Laurie. And Rebecca said, 'If you really knew what I was like, you wouldn't like me'. And so we went on, and as we talked her puppet came a bit more to life.

After the puppet exercise Rebecca began to open up more. At a subsequent session she asked, 'Do you ever watch Ellen?' referring to a popular American television series. 'Sometimes,' I replied. 'I feel awful,' she said, 'I can't tell you.' 'What would you like to tell me?' I asked gently. 'Ellen's just done something major,' she burst out. 'Something that you can relate to?' I said, knowing in my heart what I thought she was going to say. 'Yes,' replied Rebecca, almost inaudibly. 'Well, I haven't done anything,' she said softly, 'but Ellen ... Ellen said she was gay ... and I have those feelings.'

Rebecca was trying to say that she was sexually attracted to women and not interested in men. I think she was waiting for me to be absolutely horrified. 'Okay,' I said, 'so you have those feelings. How do you feel about that?'. So we explored her feelings and gradually she realized that she could talk to me and that it was okay to feel the way she did. She talked about how she couldn't possibly tell her parents and friends, because they would think she was sick. So we examined the fact that people might react in different ways, and looked at how she might deal with that.

A couple of weeks after that Rebecca was feeling a lot better, and her eating had improved. She might not have been eating regularly, but she wasn't vomiting and her depression seemed to have lifted a little. She began going to gay bars and then she met somebody. When she rang me up to tell me, she sounded so bubbly and happy.

Rebecca went on to get a job with McDonalds, and she's building up all those little stars on her uniform for being a good employee. She also plucked up the courage to tell her mum that she was gay. Her mum took the news very well, and Rebecca says she feels a huge weight has been lifted from her shoulders. Now I only see her once every couple of months – just to check how she's getting on. If she's feeling down she may not want to eat properly, but now she recognizes what's going on and will either ring the 'Caraline' helpline or work through it on her own.

Staci came to see me when she was nearly 16. Her mum phoned me initially; she was desperate. The doctor had diagnosed Staci as having bulimia nervosa. She was vomiting about thirty times a day – even if she had a cup of tea she would vomit. Often she would lock the door of the bathroom, make herself sick and pass out.

Staci came to the self-help group with her mum. Staci was very anxious – she was hot, sweaty and shaking. Her face was pale, her eyes red and sunken, her neck swollen from vomiting. She had no self-esteem and couldn't string a sentence together. She wanted to talk, but nothing she said made any sense. Later she would describe herself as feeling spaced out all the time – that's what happens when you continuously make yourself sick. She came to several counselling sessions, but was far too ill to be counselled. I was very worried about her but, because of the state she was in, I could only offer support and encourage her to come to the weekly self-help group. She was also seeing a psychiatrist at the Faringdon Wing every week, but didn't find that very helpful.

One day she came to see me in a terrible state: she was suicidal – when she went to sleep at night she hoped the morning wouldn't come. I rang the Faringdon Wing and the nurse I spoke to advised me to send her to A&E. Staci's mother took her down and, on arrival, the duty psychiatrist admitted her into the Faringdon Wing.

While she was in hospital, she attended the self-help group. She said it helped her to hear other sufferers expressing feelings she had previously thought only she had. It made her feel much less lonely.

Staci spent five and a half weeks in hospital, but when she came out she wasn't much better: she was still bingeing and vomiting. Then, one morning, she woke up and couldn't move her legs – she was numb from the waist down. Her mother called the doctor and was advised to take Staci straight to hospital, because there was a danger that her stomach was about to rupture. But Staci was petrified of going anywhere near a hospital in case she was sent back to the psychiatric ward. She refused to go. In the end, the doctor visited her at home, and told her mother that Staci's body was giving up on her. Thankfully, the sensation in her legs came back, but the whole episode shook Staci up and brought things to a head.

After that Staci left home. Because of her illness, she wasn't getting on with her parents or the younger brother she had always been so close to. It was decided that she should move out. A few of her friends said she could stay with them, but all their parents were adamant she could only stay if she stopped making herself sick. Staci had to quit vomiting or have nowhere to live. It was a struggle, but she stopped, and moved in with her best friend Sally-Ann, whose house was three minutes away from Staci's mum's.

Staci says, 'I'd hit rock bottom and hadn't died, so the only way was to float back up. I'd tried to get better before; but really only for my parents and friends because they were all so hurt watching me going through all that pain. The turning point was when I decided I wanted to do it for me, and that's when counselling started to work.'

During our sessions we explored what had triggered Staci's eating disorder. She recalled feeling depressed from the age of about eight. She went on to feel ill all the time, and sometimes she could hardly get out of bed to go to school. Eventually at 12, she was diagnosed as having an underactive thyroid, a condition that slows the metabolism. She was put on medication and there was a great deal of emphasis on weight, as every week she was weighed and had to see a dietician. Her family breathed a sigh of relief because they now knew what was wrong and her condition was being treated, but Staci didn't feel any better; she was still depressed.

Then at 15, she split up with her boyfriend. She couldn't cope and started to binge. Staci remembers the first time she made herself sick. 'One evening I had binged so much that I felt physically and emotionally sick – so I vomited. When others began to notice what I was doing it was almost as if I was saying, "Now you can *see* I am not well".'

Through counselling Staci decided she didn't want that kind of existence any more – it didn't make her happy. Little by little she reclaimed her life – finding a hairdressing job that she loved and rebuilding bridges with her family.

I hadn't seen Staci for some time when, in 1996, she turned up at a fund-raising karaoke night we were holding at the Luton Labour Club. 'Hi, Claire,' she said, 'Remember me?' I barely recognized the to-gether young woman with sparkly blue eyes. She'd given up the hairdressing job because she found it too much. She'd been on her feet all the time, working long hours and didn't get time for a lunch break. It's important for somebody like Staci to have a regular pattern, because if you haven't eaten, you are more tempted to go home and binge. She was unemployed and interested in doing voluntary work.

We took her on at 'Caraline' for a couple of months. She answered the phone, did a bit of typing and assisted me with the self-help group. Staci is amazing with people - everyone loves her, and she is excellent with clients. When the position of my personal assistant became vacant, I couldn't think of anyone more perfect for the job. Now 22, she is studying for her own certificate in counselling, and plans to become a counsellor.

When I wrote *My Body, My Enemy* I never dreamed it would be published in six languages or create the media interest it did. More people have become aware of my work and I've been nominated for one of The Prince's Trust Olay Awards for Visionary Women. The book has taken me to Denmark, and provided the spur to expand 'Caraline' into our beautiful new cen-tre, of which we are all so proud. John Butler said to me the other day, 'You can no longer be called 'Cara-line's' Project Director, because the project is com-plete. We've built the centre we hoped to, so now we'll call you Centre Director!'

On a personal note, I passed my driving test at

long last, and bought my own car. I'm still petrified of driving on the motorway though! I also decided to go to college part-time to broaden my knowledge. I now have a CSCT Advanced Certificate in Counselling Skills and Theory, and a CSCT Diploma in Therapeutic Counselling (Humanistic Route). I have branched out, and now don't solely counsel those with eating disorders.

Studying opened my mind to all sorts of therapeutic theories that I now use in my counselling. For example, if a client says they like drawing or music, I try to incorporate that interest into their therapy. I recently asked the self-help group if they would be interested in having a relaxation evening, and they all seemed keen. The following week group members bought cushions and candles and I played a relaxation CD that lasted 40 minutes. I observed my group of clients as they relaxed and the room became peaceful and still. For those 40 minutes everybody seemed to have switched off from their chaotic worlds.

Looking at the last paragraph I wrote when the book was first published in 1997, I said, 'I would be lying if I said I didn't have the odd anorexic thought; but I now understand why those thoughts happen and how to deal with them.' Three years on I can honestly say that is no longer the case. In fact, I feel so far removed from those 13 years I spent in eating-disorder hell, that if I had to write the book again from start to finish, I don't think I could. On my journey those years all seem so far away.

To contact 'Caraline', please ring our telephone helpline 01582 457474 or write to us at the following address:

Caraline: Centre for Therapy & Education
Kline House,
13 George Street West
Luton
Bedfordshire
LU1 2BJ
Our email address is caralineed@netscapeonline.co.uk
and our website is currently under development at
http://members.netscapeonline.co.uk/caralineed/

Claire Beeken 2000

Appendix 1

Useful Addresses

Childline
Freepost 1111
London
N1 0BR
0800 1111
www.childine.org.uk

The national free helpline for children and young people in trouble or danger.

Saneline
0345 678000

Helpline open from 12 noon to 2 a.m., seven days a week. Offers emotional support and information relating to mental health.

ADFAM National
Waterbridge House
32-36 Loman Street
London
SE1 0EE
0207 928 8900

Runs a national helpline for families and friends of drug users. Counselling, friendship and information about drugs and details of family support projects within the UK are available. Open from 10 a.m. to 5 p.m., Mondays to Fridays.

Eating Disorders Association
First Floor
Wensum House
103 Prince of Wales Rd
Norwich
NR1 1DW
www.edauk.com

Helpline 01603 621414 (open 9.00 a.m. to 6.30 p.m. Monday to Friday)
Youthline 01603 765050 (18 years and under. Open 4.00-6.00 p.m. Monday to Friday)
Email info@edauk.com

Maisner Centre for Eating Disorders
P.O. Box 464
Hove
East Sussex
BN3 3UG
01273 729818

Offers one-to-one consultations and postal courses for sufferers of bulimia nervosa and compulsive overeating.

Women's Therapy Centre
10 Manor Gardens
London
N7 6JS
0207 263 6200
Email info@womenstherapycentre.co.uk

Calls are answered from Monday to Thursday 10 a.m. to 12 noon and from 2 p.m. to 4.30 p.m. On Fridays, calls are answered from 10 a.m. to 12 noon. It offers feminist psychotherapy to women, individual and group therapy, and workshops on eating disorders.

Appendix 2

Recommended Reading

Bass, Ellen and Davis, Laura. *Courage To Heal – A Guide For Women Survivors of Child Sexual Abuse*, Cedar (USA), 1988

Cooper, P.J. and Fairburn, C. *Bulimia Nervosa: A Guide to Recovery*, Robinson Publishing, 1995

Crisp, A. H. *Anorexia Nervosa – Let Me Be*, Lawrence Erlbaum & Associate Publishers, updated version 1995

Dickson, Anne. *A Woman In Your Own Right*, Quartet Books, 1982

Dolan and Gitzinger. *Why Women? – Gender Issues and Eating Disorders*, Athlone Press, 1994

Duker, Marilyn and Slade, Roger. *Anorexia Nervosa and Bulimia: How to Help*, Open University Press, 1988

Schmidt, U. and Treasure, J. *Getting Better Bit(e) by Bit(e): A Survival Kit for Sufferers of Bulimia Nervosa and Binge-eating Disorders*, Psychology Press, 1996

Treasure, J. *Anorexia Nervosa: A Survival Guide for Friends, Families and Sufferers*, Psychology Press, 1997

Weiss, L. Katzman, M. and Wolchik, S. *You Can't Have Your Cake and Eat it Too: A Programme for Controlling Bulimia*. Golden Psych Press (USA) 1997

Cooper, P.J. and Fairburn, C. *Bulimia Nervosa: A Guide to REcovery*, Robinson Publishing, 1995

French, Barbara. *Coping with Bulimia*, Thorsons, 1987

Norwood, Robin. *Women Who Love Too Much*, Arrow Books Ltd, 1986